2nd Edition

Published by Headstart-UK

ISBN 0-9549146-0-0

Author: Steve Head

Publisher: Headstart UK

Editors: Jo Parfitt and Fiona Cowan of
www.SummertimePublishing.com

Design: www.plustwodesign.com

About Steve Head

At the age of four Steve was diagnosed with asthma and as this was before the days of quick relief inhalers he spent many nights gasping for air with his head over a bucket of steaming water being nursed by his probably very scared parents.

This health challenge became the cause of many missed school days.

By the time he was 16 he became the Under 19 Northumberland squash champion and today he remains a passionate sportsman as well as being a father of two, a husband and personal development coach and speaker.

As a businessman he became the number one salesman in Bayer Pharmaceuticals in 1989 after just three years with the company. Aged just 26 he was appointed as Bayer's youngest ever Area Manager.

He wouldn't describe himself as competitive but he was heard to say once, 'who wants a drawer full of second prizes?'

In 2001 he set up Headstart, a high performance coaching company following 20 years' experience as a sports coach and 16 years in sales, marketing and training.

He runs inspirational personal development programmes and delivers keynote speeches to organisations throughout the UK and Europe.

About Steve Head

Once asked who he considered to be his target audience, and knowing that everyone needs a niche, Steve responded, 'I talk to anyone with a heartbeat.' this means that he has just under 6 billion people left to work with!

His audiences so far have ranged from 13 - 65 years old.

He is known for his down to earth, humorous delivery and practical, doable approach which puts high performance and self-improvement within reach of anyone who wants it.

His intention is definitely not for you to change your life - just to make the most of the one you've got.

Steve lives with his wife Abby and his two children Christopher and Anna in Berkshire, England.

Dedication

I dedicate this book to my brother John who died on 6th November 1987 at the age of 33. He keeps me rational and reminds me every day to enjoy the things most people take for granted.

And to our twins, Stephen and Jennifer, who never saw the light of day but whose birth changed our perspective forever.

Acknowledgements

All books have acknowledgements but in this book the people I am choosing to thank are evidence that success is not a solitary journey.

Many people have had a powerful impact on my life and I am privileged to be able to recognise them now.

I thank my beautiful wife Abby for her unconditional support and love in everything I do.

My beautiful kids Anna and Christopher for their inspiration behind every story I tell.

My mam and dad for instilling in me the character to work hard and the values that give me strength every day.

To my brother Eric for always telling me the truth and helping me see things rationally and clearly.

Kriss Akabusi, Nigel Risner and Marie Mosely who came along just at the right time. I would not have a successful business without their consistent support, encouragement and friendship.

Very special thanks to Bryan Beeson for being my Number One role model and close friend who taught me to 'Just do it!!'

Paul Dawson for spotting my talent at 15 years old. You will never know how significant that was in shaping my whole life.

Arthur Williams for trusting that I was good enough in the business world well before I had any proof.

Thanks to the 100's of kids I've coached and 1000's of people who cross my path every year. Without those rich experiences I would have nothing to say.

And we couldn't have that now could we . . .

Foreword

Let me say up front that Steve Head is a personal friend and professional co-worker in the speaking and training industry. As such I could be charged with being slightly biased in my observations on this his first experience as a 'publisher of thoughts'. I promise that I have tried to be as objective as possible about a subject that can be pretty subjective.

It is my pleasure to write the foreword to Steve's publication 'How to Avoid a Near Life Experience.' I met him some five years ago at a professional speakers' association programme in London where he was a keynote speaker talking about coaching. So much of what he said resonated with my experience as a world-class athlete that we hit it off straight away. Not only did Steve and I develop a friendship but he also coached me through the fundamentals of building a workshop and working as a facilitator on my Firestarter and Be the CEO of Your Own Career programmes.

This is an easy book to read (it took me two hours without doing the exercises) and is packed with down to earth, no nonsense, gritty ideas that come not from an ivory tower but from within the workshop arena. As you leaf through the pages and work on the contents you will soon find that you have a front row seat on one of Steve Head's personal and professional development programmes. He says within the book that the Pareto Law (the 80/20 rule) applies and that 80% of people who read this will be affected in some way but that only 20% will allow the book to go to work on their life. Is this a good moment to ask in which group you will be?

Steve's experience leaps out of the page and his anecdotal evidence provides a humane background to what at times can be an ephemeral subject. In my time working with Steve I was struck by his integrity and forthrightness and I think you may feel the same.

A word of warning though! This is not a panacea, quick fix, put-it-under-your-bed-at-night-and-hey-presto-my-life-is-sorted kinda deal, but an opportunity is provided by this guide for the serious sojourner who wants to make the most of his or her three score years and 10 and leave a mark on this world.

Congratulations on being one of the many who will pick up this book. I pray that you will be one of the few to allow its contents to make a difference in your life.

C-ya and remember to 'live a life and not your fears'.

Kriss Akabusi MBE

Contents

If you want to maximise your potential and use your talents to the full, then this book is for you. In fact, if you have a heartbeat you will benefit from the ideas and strategies you are going to read about in the following pages.

I meet hundreds and thousands of people from all walks of life. I meet doctors, lawyers, accountants, sales people, nurses and computer programmers. All kinds of people. Often, at my seminars and personal development programmes, we sit and talk about dreams and aspirations. I am always amazed at how many people are just not happy. They seem to be plodding along feeling unfulfilled, somehow resigned to the fact that they will probably never get the chance to do what they really want, be who they want to be or have what they want to own. Sadly, like so many, they are waiting for their retirement or some other magical day in the future when they will get their chance to go for it. They are holding back. And apparently with good reason.

People may choose to hold back because of FEAR, or because of PEER PRESSURE and other negative influences. Or they think they are just being REALISTS, believing the risks are too great. Or they LACK CONFIDENCE or SELF-AWARENESS. Some people just simply do not believe how good or capable they really are.

But they have to justify their inaction. They develop mechanisms and excuses to keep them well and truly in their rut. They say they are too old, not educated enough, too busy, too broke, or whatever it might be. Whatever the reasons, they are always ABOUT TO DO IT, they are VERY NEARLY going to enjoy the life they deserve, but, instead, they settle for the NEAR LIFE experience they currently have.

So . . .

If you want to achieve even more success, wealth, happiness, comfort, security, fulfilment or even enhanced relationships, then you are stepping in the right direction by reading this short book. Even if you just want to be more relaxed and content this book is ideal. Just by buying this book you have already made your first move towards a more consistent performance in any area of your life that needs it.

Oh, and by the way, if you do read it all the way through you are in the top 1% of the population who on average read less than one book per year. Buying this book puts you into a very prestigious category . . . You see, you are already pretty special and you haven't even reached the end of the introduction.

Of course, having read literally hundreds of self help books and listened to as many tapes and motivational CDs, I would never suggest that this one single book is the one, but every practical idea in it I have used either as a coach or in my life personally and the results have been good to brilliant. Some of the ideas won't work for you or won't suit you, others will be exactly right.

Why bother?

Life is busy. Stress is becoming one of the major causes of sickness in the work place in the UK and USA. People, in the western world particularly, have got more than ever before - more money, more opportunity and more things - yet, as I said, most of the people I meet are feeling unfulfilled or even unhappy. They crave something else but they can't quite put their finger on what it is. But there is one thing for sure - WHAT THEY ARE DOING NOW IS NOT WORKING VERY WELL OR NOT WORKING AT ALL.

I am going to share with you here the steps you need to take if you are to become SUCCESSFUL. And if you feel that things are not that bad and that you are already enjoying some successes in your life then the ideas in this book will help you to be even more consistent and MORE SUCCESSFUL.

Through my 16 years' management experience in sales and marketing in the pharmaceutical industry, as well as the 20 years or so I have spent as a sports coach, I have learned some interesting truths about what makes certain people achieve greater levels of success than others. For reasons of simplicity I will call these people HIGH PERFORMERS. You can call them what you like, but however you think of them, the fact is some people are achieving more contentment, more wealth, more happiness and far less stress in their lives than others. Overall these people, these HIGH PERFORMERS ARE IN CONTROL of their lives and they are LOVING IT.

This doesn't mean that High Performers are not having problems or challenges. They are. It's just that, overall, they seem to be capable of more than the rest of us. They ride the challenges seemingly more effectively. They deal with failure and move on.

Are some people just naturally gifted?

Is this success something that is only available to the chosen few?

Is this success something that is only available to the chosen few?

Well, the good news is that I have identified some very simple philosophies that these high performers employ and that any one of us could, if we chose to, also apply in our own lives.

I personally have used, and continue to use, the exact ideas that you are going to read about, in my sports life, in my various jobs at Bayer and for the last three years as a self employed High Performance Coach and Speaker.

They work, every time.

Read this book if you too want to learn the ingredients that make High Performance People and how to be one. What have you got to lose?

Here is a brief outline of the High Performance Strategies you are about to explore. As I said, it's simple stuff, but honestly, you are going to need to develop a genuine passion for success in order to apply them in your own life.

How it works

I have created just 8 chapters, the first seven of which are key themes... Actually, I could have arranged them in any order because they are all of equal importance when it comes to maximising performance. Here is a brief outline of what you will find in each chapter. Feel free to read them in any order, but do ensure you read them all.

- **It's up to you**

Take responsibility for your life. If you do not accept that this is your life, you will always find an excuse. Did you know that one of the symptoms of mild depression is having a perception that life is out of your control? The sooner you accept that everything is down to you the sooner things will start to get better.

- **Know what you want**

You must begin to understand **your purpose and direction**. Having a sense of why you get out of bed and what you are aiming towards even in the short term is vital. Again, many people simply do not have any idea why they do what they do, nor do they have a passion for their work. Yet passion and purpose are key to personal motivation.

- **Expect the best**

From yourself and **set your expectations high**. There is no benefit in expecting the worst or limiting your goals or vision just in case you are disappointed. The pain of failure is no less because you planned for it.

- **Motivational fuel**

Set personal goals. I have differentiated goal setting from 'Know What You Want and Why' as this is much more specific and tangible than what I call the Purpose Principle. There are some golden rules to setting and achieving personal goals and you can learn them here.

- **Get feedback**

Increasing **self-awareness is often the first step** in self-improvement. Setting up mechanisms to gain good quality, balanced feedback is pivotal to high performance. Always be open to learn and grow.

- **Create a dream team**

No one ever achieved anything great on their own. Even Steve Redgrave never once rowed past a winning line for one of his FIVE Olympic GOLD medals, by himself. So **develop powerful support teams, minimise conflict and maximise good relationships.** Who you choose to be with, listen to, learn from and possibly model, can be life changing.

- **Model what you want**

People will treat you the way you allow them to. Becoming aware of your behaviour is crucial to your success. **The way you act** will directly affect those around you.

Now I am a practical person, so all of the ideas and tips in this book are based on practical experience. I like a bit of theory but most people I meet just want to get on with it. So I have included only the stuff that has worked for me personally and for my teams and clients . . . oh and for thousands of successful people across the world too, of course.

This is not theory, or *role play*, this is *real play*.

I will now take you through each of these themes and offer several practical exercises for you to do as you read.

I know myself that I have bought books like this and promised myself I will do this exercise or that task later but somehow I got distracted and life got too busy.

It may be worth getting a pen NOW.

Write your name on the cover of this book. Make it your book. The stuff you are going to write in it will be personal and life-changing. You don't want someone else to pick it up by mistake.

Draw on this book. Use a highlighter pen. Consider getting yourself a personal journal to capture the particularly relevant bits and to make extra notes, or to chart your progress.

So, sit up straight, with your pen in your hand and get ready to GET PRACTICAL.

By the way, my aim is not for you to change your life, just to make the most of the one you have got. I promise you all the talent you will ever need is sitting in your chair.

OK. Let's get straight to it.

Steve Head

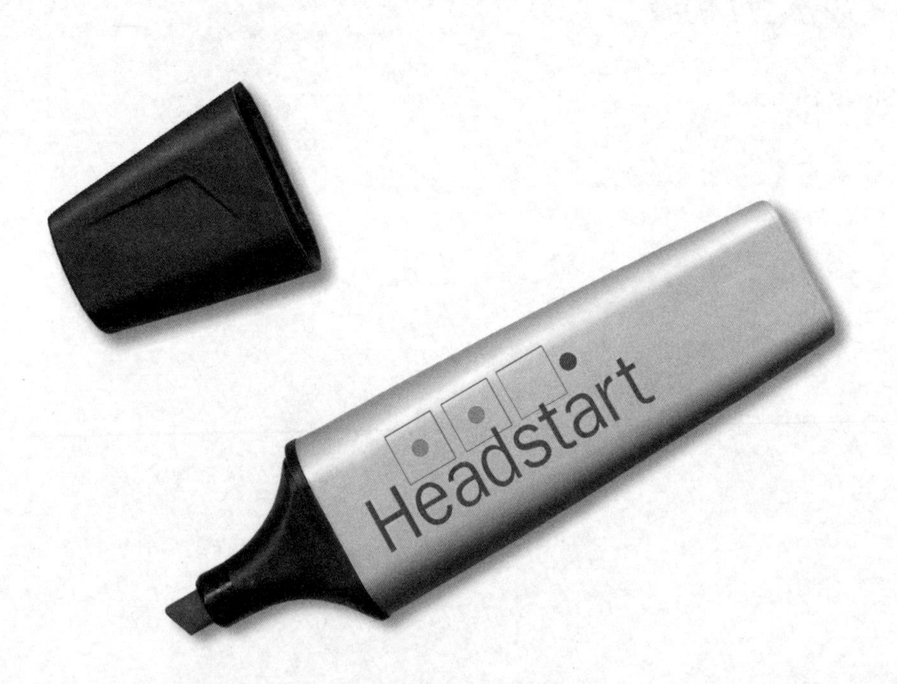
Headstart

CHAPTER 1

IT'S UP TO YOU

You are the chief executive of your life. That means you choose what you do, who you spend time with, what you eat and you choose the consequences of those choices.

Why you should read this chapter:

- **Because you need to take responsibility for your life.** If you do not accept that this is your life, you will always find an excuse.
- **Because you need to be in control.** Did you know that one of the symptoms of mild depression is having a perception that life is out of your control?
- **Because today is not a day too soon.** The sooner you accept that everything is down to you the sooner things can start to get better.

Before you get into the meat of this book please read this brief statement marked A. As you read it, consider how it makes you feel.

Statement A

You are accountable for your life . . .

Good or bad, successful or unsuccessful, happy or sad, fair or unfair, you own your life.

You are accountable, you always have been and you always will be. That may not be how you want it to be, but that is how it is.

If you don't like your job, you're accountable. If your relationships are on the rocks, you're accountable. If you are overweight, you are accountable. If you don't trust people easily, you are accountable. If you are not getting the results out of life that you feel you deserve, you are accountable.

How did it make you feel?

Did you read it and think ABSOLUTELY RIGHT! Or do you CATAGORICALLY DISAGREE!? Or do you think, perhaps WELL IT DEPENDS . . . ?

It's up to you

The funny thing is that as I travel all over the UK and EUROPE running personal development workshops with literally thousands of people from all walks of life, I ask my students the same question. I ask them how they feel about Statement A. In general everyone agrees, but it seems that there are a few conditions:

THEY WOULD PREFER IT TO READ LIKE THIS:

Statement B

Well it depends

If your life is going really well, you're accountable. If you love your job, you're accountable. If your relationships are rich, loving, caring and balanced, you're accountable.

It's a bit like bad golfers - every bad round is the weather's fault, or the club's fault or the noisy group ahead puts them off. Yet when they have the rare good round they are very happy to accept they did it themselves and were accountable

The thing is both statements (A and B) are ABSOLUTELY TRUE.

The greatest realisation that anyone can have is that YOU ARE IN CHARGE OF YOUR LIFE.

Good, bad, happy or sad it's completely down to you.

You are the chief executive of your life. That means you choose what you do, who you spend time with, what you eat and you choose the consequences of those choices.

It's up to you

So here's the thing. This book will be absolutely useless to you unless you categorically agree with both accountability statements.

So if you don't agree now and know that you never will, then you might as well put the book down and go off and do something else...

Still here?

Excellent! Then you are now assuming the mindset of the few - the High Performance mindset that is guaranteed to set you up for more success, contentment, achievement and happiness.

What's in it for you?

This book will offer suggestions and ideas that have been proven to make a difference in individual and team performance. And because most of us don't find High Performance natural we have to be disciplined to apply what we learn and take action.

So let's get something else straight right up front. **If you want an easy ride to a better richer life STOP READING this book NOW and accept that what you have is what you will probably end up with . . .**

The ideas here are simple in theory but clearly if they were all so easy to implement everyone would be doing them, wouldn't they? And they're not.

All HIGH PERFORMING, successful PEOPLE that I have met or read about, WORK REALLY REALLY REALLY HARD.

This stuff is not quick fix.

PMA

Mohammed Ali was one of the world's greatest ever sportsmen. He was possibly the definitive world champion boxer. Many remember Ali as cocky, even arrogant and egotistical. They thought he was a cheeky young man who talked a good game. In a recent documentary, Ali's coach recently said that the sportsman was the hardest working boxer he had ever met BOTH IN AND OUT OF THE RING. He trained harder, practised more and of course had INCREDIBLE self-belief.

Ali had more than just PMA, which stands for Positive Mental Attitude, by the way.

Do you think PMA is a good thing?
Of course you do.

So do I. But let's be honest, here. Having a PMA does not guarantee success. For example, if you decided to run in the 100m sprint at the Olympics right now, with no specific training, it would not matter if you had all the PMA in the world, you would still be unlikely to win. But with PMA you would probably end up a happy loser.

PMA is part of the deal but it is by no means the answer to your problems.

High Performance People make a habit of doing the things that unsuccessful people find uncomfortable.

Over the years, I have met thousands of amazing people with AWESOME natural talent. Yet few of them fulfil their potential and many never even recognise their gifts. They simply go unused.

In fact, most people appear to be having what I would call NEAR LIFE EXPERIENCES.

They are always about to make the big change, but somehow life is just too busy. They think they will get round to doing it TOMORROW.

If anyone ever says 'I'll start my training tomorrow', or 'I'll give up smoking next week,' they are not committed. If it's worth doing it's worth doing NOW!

IWIN Disease (I Want It Now)

You know, this is not rocket science. The things that make a real difference in your life are remarkably easy to understand and they lie well within your grasp right now. But there is one big catch:

Most of us are 'bone idle'

Have you noticed how many people seem to want an easy route to success and financial freedom? They will happily buy a product called Slim Quick because they are convinced it will resolve their weight problems, yet deep down they know that slimming is a combination of dedication, attitude, support, discipline, drive and motivation. It takes time to reach a target weight, to adjust a metabolism, to change a lifestyle. And even though they know that all this EFFORT AND HARD WORK will probably reduce their cardiovascular risks and give them more energy for a longer life, they still buy Slim Quick. Come on!

They aren't daft, just lazy!!!

High Performance People make a habit of doing the things that unsuccessful people find uncomfortable.

80/20

I expect you will have heard of the Pareto 80/20 theory before.

In simple terms it says that 80% of profits, results, inventions or whatever comes from 20% of the population. This law holds true in every environment I have encountered through my work and leisure.

When I run my seminars, after the students have had three days learning motivational and practical ideas on performance, I ask the following question:

> *Based on Pareto's law I know that only 20% of you will actually do anything different when you leave this seminar.*
>
> *Show me by raising your hand if you will be in that 20%.*

Guess what? Every hand goes up. Yet I know that the law will hold true.

80% will do nothing different. They will do *diddlysquat*.

Every day, thousands of books like this one are bought (though not read necessarily). People listen to CDs and attend seminars all the time, yet very few of them actually do anything different as a result.

Why should this be?

As I said earlier, WE CRAVE FOR SOMETHING MORE. But somehow we just can't be bothered to go and get it. It's somehow easier to settle for what we have and live a NEAR LIFE experience.

Consider this:

> *You will probably live for 80 years based upon current medical developments. If you NEARLY do what you really want for the rest of your life how will you feel?*

If the Pareto Principle is true then you will need to make an effort if you want to be in that 20%. A bit of effort is all it takes. And you may spend the rest of your 80 years enjoying even more happiness and fulfilment, which you deserve by the way.

I was recently on holiday in France and spent some time with the Manager of our travel company. Peter was only 21 but was easily the most professional holiday company representative I have ever met.

My car had developed a problem with the brakes and Peter had willingly gone the extra mile, and taken me to the local garage himself to organise a swift service at a good price. On the way he told me about his interview when he first joined his company when he had been just 18 years old.

Peter's mother had bought him a posh suit so he would look his best (he spent two years paying her back!). He had prepared a file of his achievements and successes. He had rehearsed all the questions and answers he could think of. Peter was ready.

As he waited with the other would-be employees at the interview he had been amazed at their apparent lack of preparation. No suits in sight, no smart presenter folders. They looked as if they did not care. Half way through his interview Peter was told that he was the best candidate they had ever seen. They wanted him to have the job and were sorry that they had to put up a pretence as they conducted the remaining interviews. Just by looking at the others, they could tell Peter was the person they wanted.

What did Peter do that was so amazing? He just went the extra mile. In fact it was probably less than that. He just made a bit of effort, when no one else had made any at all. It really doesn't take much to get more of what you want and need.

About seven years ago I had this bizarre idea of leaving the corporate world and becoming a full time professional speaker and coach. I made it my mission to read every book I could find on motivation, performance, coaching and success. I aimed to read 50 per year (so far so good). I also read business journals, sales and marketing magazines, I attended seminars to see and hear the best speakers in the world on performance, personal and business success.

This meant that I had to travel all over the UK and even to the USA. I was prepared to give up some of my weekends to attend seminars and mastermind groups (more of these in Chapter 6) too. And you must understand that this is a big sacrifice for me as my weekends are hugely valuable to me as this is Family and Golf Time!!!!

I wanted to become an expert in my subject.

It's up to you

The difference between what I do and all the others who strive for their own successes and achievements is not that I am somehow gifted, more intelligent, or even better looking. It's just that I am prepared to get up earlier, maybe go to bed later and actually apply the learning. In addition, bit by bit, step by step I actually do something with the information I acquire. I apply the steps outlined in this book and they just work. Even in my marriage.

Luck has nothing to do with it.

Oh and by the way you're not lucky when you suddenly seem to achieve greater levels of success and happiness. I heard a quote many years ago that is absolutely spot on:

Luck is what happens when great planning meets with opportunity.

So put in the time and you will reap the results. Trust me.
And so onto the High Performance, non-rocket-science-but-difficult-to-do high performance stuff.

Luck is what happens when great planning meets with opportunity.

SIXTY SECOND SUMMARY

- *It's up to you. You are responsible for your life.*
- *Too many people have lots of untapped potential and dormant talent.*
- *Many people are frustrated by their current situation but have resigned themselves to putting up with what they have.*
- *Fear of change, fear of the unknown or fear of failing are common excuses that we give ourselves to justify inaction.*
- *Many people are not prepared to work hard for the success they crave. They are hoping that some day, things might just get better, relying on luck to shape their lives.*
- *High Performance People:*
  - *. Acknowledge that they are in charge of their own destiny.*
  - *. Know that PMA is helpful though real happiness and fulfilment is a product of working really hard and expecting the best.*
  - *. Believe they have untapped talent and potential.*
  - *. Too many people are having near life experiences.*

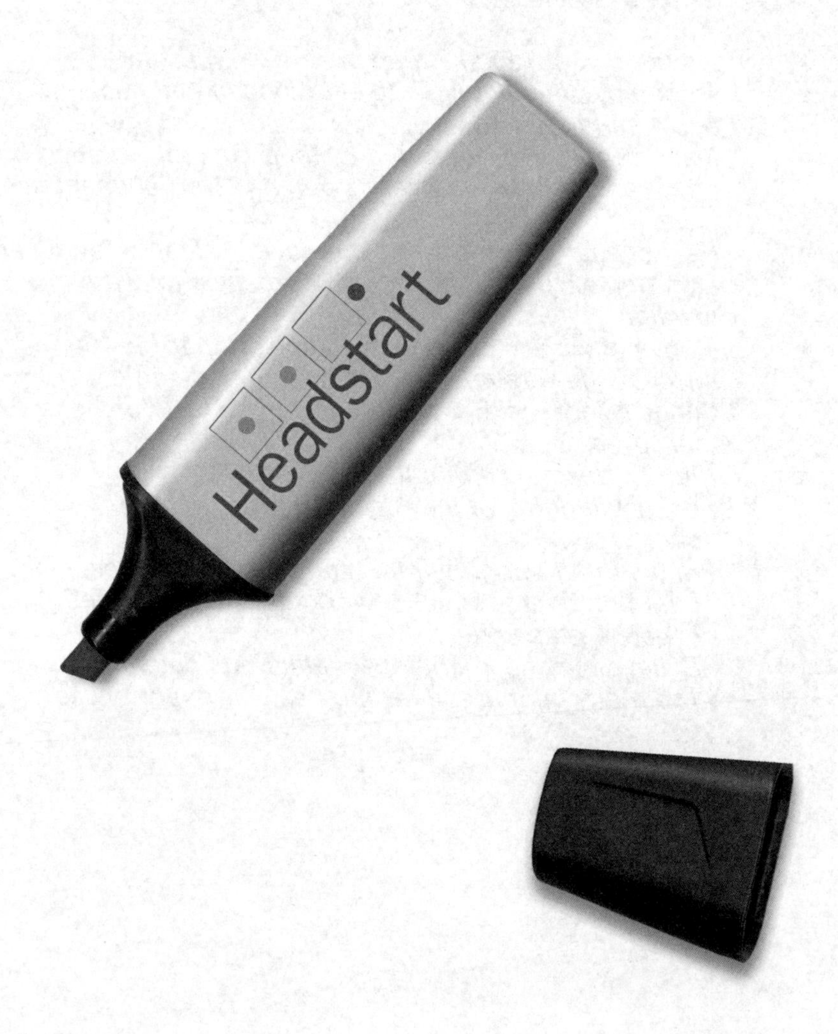
Headstart

CHAPTER 2

KNOW WHAT YOU WANT

Think about this for a moment: most people spend more time planning their holidays than they do planning their lives.

Why you should read this chapter:

- **Because you need to understand your purpose and direction.** Having a sense of why you get out of bed and what you are aiming towards even in the short term is vital. Again, many people simply do not have any idea why they do what they do, nor do they have a passion for their work.

- Because **passion and purpose are key** to personal motivation.

It's cool to be busy

The majority of people I meet are doing pretty well for themselves.

They are busy most of the time, either working or rushing from one event to the next. But the big questions for most of are:

Q Are we really HAPPY? Are we enjoying the moment? Are we getting what we want? Really?

Q Are we engaged in activity that fulfils us and gives us a sense of peace and contentment?

Q Or are we living life on the basis that HAPPINESS IS A DESTINATION and that on some magical day at a certain time in the future we will arrive at that dream destination? But only if we are lucky!!!

Q Do you just HOPE that everything will fall into place like the pieces of a completed jigsaw puzzle. Do you hope that all of this 'busyness' will have been worthwhile?

Millions of people every week buy a lottery ticket on the basis that a lucky win will make them happy! In other words these people are relying on luck to deliver their happiness!

Yet despite all this 'busyness' we often find ourselves at the end of a working week feeling tired but with no real sense of fulfilment.

Why is this?

Consider how you spent the last month. Ask yourself how you used your time? Were you busy? I bet you were. But more importantly did you feel fulfilled? Did you feel that all that effort and racing around was worthwhile?

Or were you just busy having a NEAR LIFE experience.

Having a sense of purpose

> *'It is not eminent talent that is required to ensure success in any pursuit, so much as purpose - not merely the power to achieve but the will to labour energetically and perseveringly.'*
> *- Samuel Smiles*

Samuel Smiles wrote the above lines in his groundbreaking book *'Self Help'* way back in 1859. During my personal development seminars I often ask people to think about their life purpose. Most of them find this daunting.

Think about this for a moment: most people spend more time planning their holidays than they do planning their lives.

Most couples spend more time planning their wedding day than the marriage, which they hope will last a lifetime.

Now I said this was going to be practical . . .

Before we can go any further, let's stop for a moment and think about what you want to do with your life - and perhaps more importantly, why you want it. This will help you find your purpose and direction.

My favourite things

Try this simple exercise, below. Don't spend more than a few seconds on it. Just go with your first instinctive thoughts.

Answer the following questions and for each just note down one or two examples and certainly no more than three.

Know what you want

List the jobs you have done that carry the most positive memories for you.

____

____

List the hobbies you have enjoyed during your life that you think about with positive memories. When you did them you lost all sense of time.

____

____

List the times when using your gifts or talents have given you the most amazing memories.

____

____

List what you consider to be your most significant life experiences. Maybe they happened on holiday, when you were a child at school, or even more recently.

____

____

Now think of a childhood photo that carries wonderful memories for you. Make a note of what were you doing and who you were with at the time.

____

____

Look back at your answers. Can you spot any themes or patterns that run through your answers? Maybe they hold a clue to your passions? You may see that sport, music, family, being outdoors or mixing with people are regular themes for you. Make a note of recurring themes here:

____

____

'Happiness is the number one goal of most people and yet the majority (up to 73 per cent) have no idea of what would actually bring them this so-called happiness, or indeed have any sense of direction in life.' - Dave Pelzer.

The state of flow

Mihaly Csikszentmihalyi is a leading psychologist and business guru. His book, 'Flow' was addressing this life purpose issue or the meaning of life. He wrote:

'People in a state of flow feel that they are engaged in a creative unfolding of something larger; athletes call it 'being in the zone' mystics have described it as 'ecstasy' and artists term it 'rapture'. You and I may recognise our flow experiences as simply those that seem to make time stand still.

Perception and understanding have come to a stop and spirit moves where it wants.

In simple terms you stop thinking and just do.'

Are there any activities that you get involved in now or used to enjoy, which have this effect on you? If so, then take notice. These moments are rare, but when they happen you are being given a glimpse of your essence of purpose, or at least a basic talent or gift.

Being a practical kind of person myself, as you can expect, I have done the above exercise too. I learned that my top three themes were music, sport and people. I then asked myself whether I was engaging in these activities regularly in some way. For me, my work is involved with people. I play squash and golf weekly and work with sportsmen and coaches too. As I am not a musician, putting music into my life takes a bit more effort. So, once a month, we hire a babysitter and go out to enjoy some live music.

A sense of purpose

Dave Pelzer is the author of 'A Child Called It'. He experienced the third worst case of child abuse in the history of the State of California. Now he spends his time counselling others and working with children. He has learned some frightening statistics:

'Happiness is the number one goal of most people and yet the majority (up to 73 per cent) have no idea of what would actually bring them this so-called happiness, or indeed have any sense of direction in life.' – Dave Pelzer.

Know what you want

Having a clear sense of purpose and meaning is crucial if you are to have a hope of achieving happiness. We all need focus. We need to be productive.

If you have ever watched Big Brother, I'm a Celebrity - Get Me Out of Here, or other similar reality TV programmes where people are shut up together in a confined space for several weeks, then you know what happens. They start to get introspective and moan a lot. They complain about each other. In Big Brother particularly, they also stop getting out of bed. With no purpose or structure to their days they lose motivation and start to vegetate. Once they realise that each day is totally predictable they sleep more and do less.

Some people create their own Big Brother experience.

High Performers do things very differently.

What makes them different?

So what is the magic ingredient that makes successful people different? People like Kelly Homes, David Beckham, JK Rowling, Tiger Woods, Steve Redgrave, or Bill Gates?

Jonny Wilkinson was instrumental in England's recent World Championship win. Like many High Performers he is:

Committed to a specific purpose and Works much harder than those that would aspire to be as good

This means practising longer and harder, sometimes alone, even during holidays.

It is interesting to learn that during that epic final against Australia in November 2003, during the interval and just before the match went to extra time, Sir Clive Woodward was trying to psyche the team up for the last few minutes.

'I'm just going to go and practise my kicking, then,' said Jonny.

Clive couldn't believe it. Surely of all people Jonny Wilkinson would not need to practise at such a crucial point in the biggest match of his life?

The match was decided by a last minute kick.

You can probably guess who converted!

Lance Armstrong, the six times winner of the Tour de France and survivor of testicular cancer has also proved the point. Lance is living proof that determination is crucial to success. The Tour De France is a 2290 mile road race and is rated as the most gruelling sports event on the planet. He goes through considerable pain to achieve his superhuman results.

In his book *'It's Not About the Bike'*, he highlights the reality of his success.

> ***'I've read how I "flew up the Mountains and hills of France," but you don't fly up a hill, you struggle slowly and painfully up a hill and maybe if you work very hard you get to the top you get there before everybody else,' he writes.***

Lance also has a great mantra:

> ***'Pain is temporary but quitting lasts a lifetime,'- Lance Armstrong.***

Kriss Akabusi is a friend and colleague of mine. He is an astounding example of someone who has a tremendous sense of what he is about. You may know him best for his world-class hurdling or his time on television, presenting Record Breakers. But did you know that he started his career in the Army and is now one of the best professional speakers in the UK?

Kriss has had several concurrent careers, each as hugely successful as the one before. Each time that he starts a new career he decides what he wants to be, by when, and then whom he needs to speak to in order to help him get there.

People walk up to Kriss and say: 'It's OK for you, you're a celebrity. You are Kriss Akabusi.' But this High Performance Person came to England as an orphan. He has achieved everything through dedication and desire. It is important that we remember to keep our perspective. If Kriss has been helped at all, it is only by his ability to be focused, quite naturally, on getting what he wants. He sets his goals one at a time, depending on the talents he wants to use at that precise moment.

He also has a driving purpose A BIG WHY? He is crystal clear why he gets out of bed in the morning and he is highly successful as a result. By that I mean, Kriss is happy, chilled out and great fun to be with. And in case you are thinking it must be because he's well off, I know many people much wealthier than Kriss who are downright miserable.

Believe me it's NOT THE MONEY that makes the difference.

We could all do with a role model like these characters, described above.

We could all do with a dose of Kriss Akabusi or Lance Armstrong's thinking to help us on our life journey.

Get perspective

I recently worked with groups of 14 year olds in a local school. As you may know getting 14 year olds to pay attention for more than a few minutes can be difficult.

This is how I began:

"If the world was a village and everything was scaled down to same ratios but the population was just 100, this is how things would pan out:

57 of the 100 would be Asian
21 of the 100 would be European
14 of the 100 would be from the Western Hemisphere
8 of the 100 would be African
52 of the 100 would be female
48 of the 100 would be male
70 of the 100 would be non white
30 of the 100 would be white
70 of the 100 would be Non-Christian
30 of the 100 would be Christian
6 of them would possess 59% of the world's wealth
80 of them would live in substandard housing
70 of the 100 would not be able to read
50 of the 100 would suffer from malnutrition
1 of the 100 would be near death
1 of the 100 would be being born
1 only would have an education
1 only would have a computer"

This means that you are one of 60 million most privileged people in the world today.

Those teenagers all listened, really well.

I then asked how many of them had a car in the family and every hand went up. I asked how many had two cars and again, every hand stayed up . . .

I still had their attention.

If nothing else, the scenario described above gives us a sense of context. It reminds us that we are in a great position to make something of ourselves. It removes a lot of excuses.

What is success?

So, what does success mean for you? Did you get out of bed this morning unaided? That's a success. Did you dress yourself unaided? That's a success. Did you get your own breakfast and feed yourself? That's a success. It would have been for my brother John.

John was born in 1954 on Guy Fawkes' night. Unknown to him he would spend his whole life coping with a physically debilitating form of Cerebral Palsy, which would rob him of his co-ordination and balance.

His life was a roller coaster of happy times and deep depressions; complaining, however was something very alien to John.

As if life were not challenging enough, in April 1987, John was diagnosed with an advanced form of Leukaemia and was given only three months to live. His deterioration was marked and rapid yet still no complaints, just a refusal to lie down and give in.

He smiled most days. And even lost his sight two days before he passed away. No complaints. He forgot to mention it.

Finally, John died on the 6th of November; 33 years and one day since his birth.

John gave his family a unique insight and perspective on life.

He inspired us to live life to the full and taught the real meaning of courage.

He was and still is a hero. Someone whose story can give us all perspective and context.

John could easily count ten, 20 or 30 successes in any one day. Getting out of bed was a success for him.

You may dream of getting a gold medal in the Olympics. That is a goal that few of us are ever likely to attain. John dreamed of being able to feed himself.

Success is different for everyone. Success also depends on the context.

Do you have a credit card? Imagine taking it out of your wallet and holding it. That card gives you access to money, it can pay your bills, it will let you borrow money and even buy a holiday or a car. I bet you have some loose change on you too.

Could you go into a church or place of worship at some point today? Without fear? Chances are, you know you could go there without being persecuted for your beliefs.

The fact that you have access to money and can go into a place of worship puts you in the top one per cent of the world's population.

This means that you are one of 60 million most privileged people in the world today

If you can also read, and I would guess you can, that puts you in the top half a per cent.

Now how do you feel about the word success?

Let me talk about sport again for a moment. Did you know that 90 per cent of the issues that people face on a squash court have nothing to do with their ability to play the game? In fact, the problems people face when playing any sport or indeed facing any business or personal challenge, arise because they do not feel positive about themselves or their ability.

Imagine you were to sit down right now and talk for 30 minutes to a person sitting next to you about all the things that have gone wrong in your life, and all the mistakes you have made. I'll bet that 30 minutes would not be enough. In fact moaning and whining are two things that most of us are well practised at, so much so that most meetings would last half as long if moaning, complaining and whining were banned.

Now, let's say I ask you to sit knee to knee, eye to eye with someone - and tell them about all the things you love and admire about yourself. You would be hard pressed to think of a single thing to say.

Trust me, I do this exercise on my High Performance Programmes and you can literally feel the discomfort. People react almost with shock. When I ask how they feel they use words like, uncomfortable, speechless, dread, fear, cold sweat, nightmare, I've gone blank and so on. One guy actually got up and ran to the loo. Yeah right . . .

Even when I ask people to take a piece of paper and just write down a list of all the successes they have ever had in their lives. Yes, I don't mean in the last year, I mean ever, most people find that really hard. Maybe not as hard as sitting knee to knee with a complete stranger and saying what you do well, but difficult all the same.

I often ask my students to list 10 successes in 30 seconds. That is 10 successes in their lives so far. Some of them barely write one thing in that time. Next, I tell them a story about my brother John, or about being in the top half a per cent of all the people in the world. Then I give them another 30 seconds. I challenge them to write ten things down by then. It is still tough, but it gets better. So then I tell them another story, and give them another 30 seconds and it gets easier still. Some people have actually written ten or 20 things by then.

Could you?

Take 30 seconds, just 30 seconds and write down your successes that you have had since you were born.

____

____

____

____

____

____

____

____

Start a success log

Here's another practical idea to help you:

Now I am really lucky because in my role as a trainer, coach and inspirational speaker I get loads of feedback and testimonials. I keep them all in a file, in fact a few files. If ever I feel a little unsure about an up and coming challenge I just read some of the positive comments from my Success Log.

I would strongly recommend you have one. Start it now. Make a note to buy yourself a file or folder the next time you are in town. The 10 successes you wrote down earlier are just the beginning.

Imagine it. If you were to write down one of your successes every day, within a year you would have 365. The next time you have a big presentation to make or a difficult meeting to attend or any challenge at all, read your list. I guarantee it will give you five per cent more confidence at least.

> *Tip*
> *You may want to buy a really expensive journal so that this exercise has even more value and purpose.*

Success statement

Often, I ask my delegates to think not only about their own successes and achievements, but also about what success means to them.

Something odd happens at this point. Whenever I ask them to do this, they never write down things like: 'I want to win £50 million'.

No, they usually write that they want a reasonable amount of comfort, enough money in the bank, interesting experiences, to travel and to have more freedom and to be with the people they love.

Then I read about people like Sir Clive Woodward, Bill Gates or Sir Richard Branson. It is obvious that they are all focused on creating an impact and have become an inspiration to us all. Yet the force that drives these people, amazing people, is made up of the same kind of ambitions that you would write down in your own Success Statement. I'll be helping you with yours a little later in this chapter.

These people too wanted good relationships, freedom and comfort rather than a tangible outcome such as Virgin, Microsoft or winning a gold medal. They have a genuine desire to make a difference.

I come from Newcastle. While I was growing up, nothing came easy. The only things handed to me on a plate were love and affection. Today, I have a really comfortable lifestyle.

It's not about having money, if it was then all rich people would be happy

I'm sure you can think of many sad, rich people. For me, success is something different: I can suggest, at the drop of a hat, that we all go away for a week's holiday abroad. I can take four weeks off in the summer to go to France with the family. I don't just get to do this kind of thing once a year - in fact in my business plan I have a commitment to 12 weeks holiday a year. I can do it almost any time. I work almost exclusively during term time, so I can spend more quality time with the children during their holidays. This is my rule book for life. This is my definition of success. What's yours?

Finding your flow

We are all made up of many roles, or parts. The worker, or career person, is just one of those parts. We may be a mother, a wife, a writer, a husband, a son. Listen to the words you use when you describe yourself. You don't say: 'I do husbanding,' or: 'I do fathering'. You say: 'I am a father,' or: 'I am a husband.'

Similarly, I don't say: 'I do coaching'. I say: 'I am a coach'.

In fact if I were to list who I am, right now I would say that I am a father, a husband, a professional speaker, a high performance specialist and a sportsman.

I feel totally absorbed when I'm involved in any of these roles I lose track of time I am in the FLOW.

Where do you feel IN THE FLOW?

You need to start noticing what makes you feel brilliant. But you also need to be aware of how much time you spend involved in those things. Usually it's nowhere near as much as you'd like or deserve, I suspect.

Know what you want

Lots of people need help to identify what they love to do. It's a mistake to think you have to give a definitive answer. It is OK not to know what you love to do when you are a teenager. When I work with teenagers in schools I like to remind them that it is OK at 15 not to know what they want to do yet. But I tell them that it is important that they start noticing the stuff that comes easy.

Have you noticed that children today, especially teenagers, do not voice their ambitions for desk bound jobs and high salaries?

They shun the rat race. They have watched their parents work their hearts and souls out yet aren't enjoying the experience or the results - and they don't want to repeat the pattern. They can see that there is no balance in their parents' lives. You should ask yourself whether today's teenagers are just lazy, or whether they have a point. Evening TV is filled with programmes about people relocating to France or Spain. They want to slow down, and begin living life ON PURPOSE.

When you are doing something that you love, you will do your very best. You will notice that things feel different while you are doing them. You will be like Billy Elliot, in the film, who can only explain how dancing makes him feel by saying: 'I just kind of disappear.'

Often you will realise that you have a talent or a gift for doing something, only because it feels so easy, so effortless. When you feel energised by something you love, you need not only to recognise that but also to find a way to recreate it.
Ellen MacArthur in her book *'Taking On The World'*, said that as a teenager she was literally up to her arms in resin as she submerged herself in yachting, weather systems, radio communications and construction. She said 'I was learning and I was loving it.'

Doing it, learning it, being totally submerged in something is another way of getting close to PURPOSE.

It's not about having money, if it was then all rich people would be happy.

Know what you want

In the book *'Now Discover Your Strengths'* by Marcus Buckingham and Don Clifton they suggest that any activity that fulfils the criteria of learning, yearning or satisfaction would indicate a strength, talent and possible purpose:

- **Yearning**
  Do you have a yearning that you have had since being a child? Is there anything that you may have put on hold because life got in the way? Don't keep ignoring it. Look for opportunities to use it.

- **Learning**
  Do you find there are some things you just love to learn about? I mean anything. And like Ellen the learning is easy. You would gladly read a book without stopping or travel 10000 miles to be involved in a seminar on the subject.

- **Satisfaction**
  Are their any activities that cause you to lose all sense of time and be in FLOW when you engage in them?

If you can think of an activity or passion you have which lets you put a big tick beside all three criteria you are one step closer to being ON PURPOSE.

Take a risk

I don't think you have a hope of knowing truly what you love to do, or want to do with your life, until you have tried things. A wide range of things. It's OK to try things out, as long as they are safe and don't harm anybody. If you try something new you may find that you don't enjoy doing it. That's all part of the learning experience too, and very necessary.

Our kids are brilliant at trying things especially new food. They take great pride in telling Abby and me how they at least tried it even if they never eat it again. Interestingly, their diet is varied and exotic. They will eat anything from spicy Thai curry to smoked salmon.

Billy Connolly was being interviewed on the Parkinson show recently. He was talking about his life and getting older. He said the greatest word in the English Language is YES!!! Just say yes more often. Every time your instinct is to hold back, walk away or wait for another day, do YES instead.

In *'The Legend of Bagger Vance'* the actor Will Smith plays the part of caddy to the golfer played by Matt Damon. At one point Damon is scrabbling around in the bushes looking for the ball, when he says: 'Every one of us is born with an authentic swing.' Whether you like it or not you have a natural talent or gift you just need to acknowledge it and nurture it.

Each and every one of us has an authentic swing. We just have to acknowledge it and nurture it.

Tip
By the way your homework is to watch 'The Legend of Bagger Vance'.

In *'Sleepless in Seattle'*, Tom Hanks plays the part of a single father who is looking for a new girlfriend, and whose son is getting tired of his father's exploits. Hanks explains to his son that he is just trying out new things to see if he likes them. You could do that too.

Purpose Awareness Exercise

We have talked a lot about success and now I would like you to take a few minutes to write your Success Statement. Think for a few minutes about all the things that make up your Life Purpose.

Consider your:

- Talents
- Strengths
- Flow experiences
- The things you love to learn
- The things you yearn for
- The things that give you satisfaction
- Your authentic swing
- What makes you happy
- What you 'do'
- Your successes
- Your achievements

Write down your definition of success - what success means to you. Picture it in your mind. Describe what would have to be happening for you to know this was success. Write down what would define that? What would you own? Where would you be? Who would you be with? How would you spend your days at work, your days off, and your holidays?

Know what you want

Success for me is

Each and every one of us has an authentic swing. We just have to acknowledge it and nurture it.

SIXTY SECOND SUMMARY

- *Having a sense of purpose is something that motivates and drives us.*

- *Identifying your favourite things will highlight the important things in your life and remind you of purposeful activities.*

- *Mihaly Csikszentmihalyi describes Flow as a state where you are totally engaged in an experience and you lose track of time.*

- *Notice when you are IN THE FLOW.*

- *Money is not the secret of everlasting happiness, if it were then all rich people would be happy.*

- *Say YES more often.*

- *The three key indicators of life purpose:*

- *Yearning*
- *Learning*
- *Satisfaction*

- *Success is different for everyone. Defining success for you will bring you one step closer to living life on purpose.*

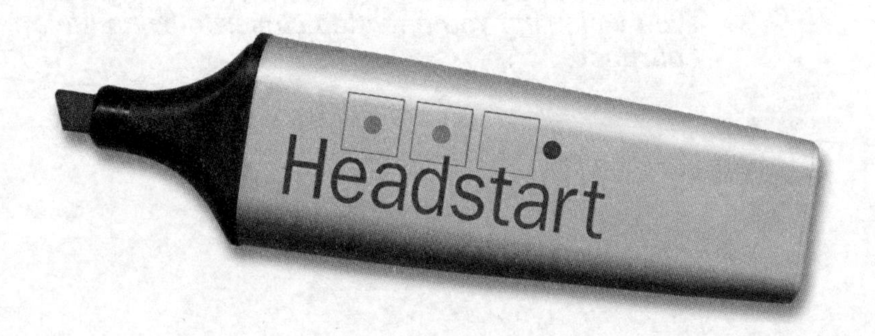
Headstart

CHAPTER 3

EXPECT THE BEST

People like this aren't ill, they've just practised misery too long and they're getting used to it . . .

Why you should read this chapter:

- **Because there are significant benefits in expecting success.**
- Because **negative thinking limits** your chances of getting what you deserve.
- Because **expecting failure doesn't make it any easier** to cope with if it happens.
- Because there are **practical techniques** in this chapter that you can learn to apply that will set you up for even more contentment and fulfilment.

You may as well set yourself up for success.

I am constantly amazed by people who lower their sights so that they are aiming to achieve mediocrity and then complain because someone else has more than they have.

In fact some people go one step further and actually sabotage their likelihood of success.

Self Handicapping

Some people sabotage their success on purpose. Believe it or not self-handicapping is a self-limiting strategy that is recognised by psychologists.

This concept was studied extensively during the 80's and 90's. It has been discovered that self-handicappers create an excuse for their poor performance. For example, they may stay out late before an important test. In this way they create themselves a 'genuine' reason for their possible failure.

This strategy is designed to protect their self-esteem. Its motive can be either personal or public. This means that you protect yourself from both private and public ridicule.

Again, if you are interested in High Performance you need to recognise this kind of self-destruct mechanism and deal with it. By the way . . .

People like this aren't ill, they've just practised misery too long and they're getting used to it . . .

Self-awareness

The first step you need to take towards self-improvement is to acknowledge that something actually needs changing or improving. You see, it does not matter how many solutions people may offer you to a problem situation, if you do not accept that you have a problem, then you will not take notice of the solutions. Until you believe there is a problem you will do absolutely nothing about it.

Take a good hard look at yourself and be honest.

In Figure 3.1 I have created a simple exercise to get you thinking. For each of the points below rank them in terms of importance on a scale of 1 - 10, with 1 low and 10 high. Write the appropriate number in each circle.

Now rank the same items in terms of how you think you are doing right now. Again, rank them between 1 and 10.

Now you will have two numbers in each circle. See how your expectations compare with your reality.

The Life Wheel

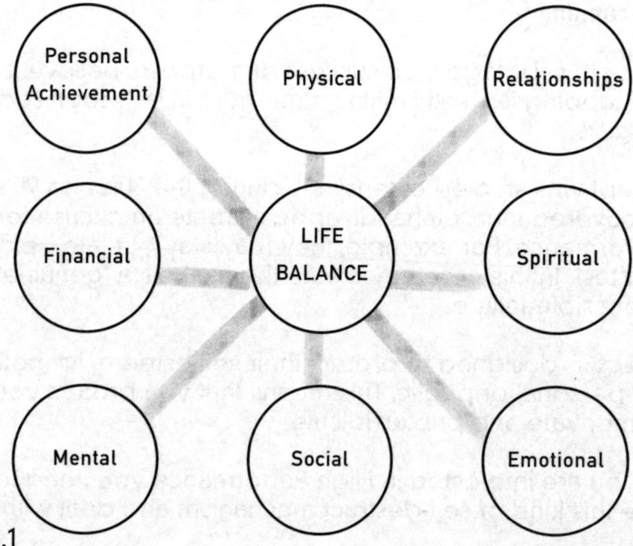

Figure 3.1

Expect the best

This exercise is a simple self-awareness status report. Use it to identify right away where you need to put in most effort. From my experience I know that success has a lot to do with self-esteem, self-awareness and having that sense of purpose I talked about earlier.

It is hard to know what you want until you are crystal clear about who you are.

Our self-esteem enables or disables us in our quest for highly productive relationships and success.

Your self-awareness allows you to understand your own behaviour and why you do the things you do.

In his book *'Emotional Intelligence'*, author, Daniel Goleman clearly identifies the foundation of high performance behaviour as self-awareness.

Being brilliant

I use another exercise to help with this. Initially this was an exercise I only did at home with the kids, but it has evolved to be a very powerful experience for company executives and staff.

If you watch any world-class athlete or sports person you can virtually guarantee that this concept will have been used in one form or another. It is the fundamental philosophy behind High Performance Coaching. Focusing on strengths rather than weaknesses will always give better results. And I mean always.

It goes like this when we do it at home:

We take it in turns to speak, as we go round the table, each saying a sentence that begins with the words 'I am brilliant at . . .'

Anna usually goes first:

'I am brilliant at colouring in,' she says.

Then Christopher has to add to Anna's list.

He might say Anna is brilliant at 'Eating her veg'.

Abby will add her comment and finally it's my turn.

Then it's Christopher's turn and so on . . .

'Don't waste time trying to input new stuff, draw out the talent that is already there.'

The game continues round and round the table as we all consciously acknowledge each other's strengths.

We used to call the game the *'What are you good at'* game but it is now affectionately known as Moments of Brilliance, or MOB for short. It is a winner every time.

Tip
Warning!!!!! Please do try this at home; seriously it will cost you nothing.

If you have ever had a performance appraisal, almost certainly you will have experienced the deflating feeling as someone tells you how well you are doing, only to go on to say the inevitable however or but followed by 'you have several areas for development' (they mean weaknesses). Then they go on to create a development plan focusing on your limitations.

In the excellent book *'First Break All The Rules'*, a study of over 80,000 high performing, managers from all over the world highlighted one consistent theme. Just one! My simplified version of this is . . .

'Don't waste time trying to input new stuff, draw out the talent that is already there.'

Noticing weaknesses is easy to do but really hard to do anything about. This was the primary insight from 25 years of research by Gallup. Simply pointing out weaknesses boils down to damage limitation. At best it will give you OK results. Drawing attention to the negatives is out of date and ineffective. Start drawing out the good stuff instead.

Inner voice

We all have an Inner Voice and most of us use it ineffectively to say the least. Instead of giving ourselves regular pep talks and praise we focus on disappointments and worries. We become very good at self-criticism.

I run this following exercise in all my workshops and keynotes, or something similar. I call it Talking Nicely to You. You could call it Do Your Own MOB if you like.

So, just for 30 seconds I would like you to talk to yourself about your strengths, gifts and talents.

Ideally if you have a relative or friend close at hand who can spare you a minute, then work together.

Notice how comfortable it is to talk about yourself in this way. Or should I say how 'uncomfortable'? Think of everything you LOVE about yourself. Focus on your uniqueness, your real talents.

From my experience TOO MANY PEOPLE PRACTISE MISERY most of their lives and become very, very good at it.

And by the way you are not allowed to talk about your children or partner during this exercise. This is about you personally. This is soul-searching stuff.

So, shut the book now and do this exercise right away.

The majority of people are dumb-struck at the very thought of doing this exercise.

If someone spoke to you the way you talk to yourself you'd probably slap him or her!

This exercise is a first step in getting you to talk nicely to you.

Practise success

The power of your inner voice must not be underestimated.

Conventional thinking says that success creates optimism but as Martin Seligman, the author of *'Learned Optimism'*, shows the reverse is true. On a regular, repeated basis optimism tends to deliver success.

Seligman wrote his book in 1991. He found that people who give up and fail to achieve success never dispute their failures. Yet those who regularly overcome adversity listen to their internal dialogue, challenge any limiting thoughts and even find positive reasons for rejection.

In short they become BRILLIANT AT PRACTISING SUCCESS. They train their inner voice to be supportive, constructive and kind. High Performance People are really good at this.

Expect the best

If you want to succeed, you must believe it with every cell of your body and use the language of success both to yourself and to others.

I don't mean that you need to become arrogant and big headed. I simply mean that you should stop being self-destructive, quit the negative talk and give yourself a fighting chance of fulfilling your potential.

'Whether you think you can or you think you can't. you're right.'
– Henry Ford

Think of Tiger Woods for a moment. People have an instant image of him in their minds when they think of him, don't they? They think of someone tall and smartly dressed, probably wearing black trousers, black shoes and even a red shirt. He brands himself like a success from top to toe. And then he speaks with the language of success too.

'The guy beat me,' he says. 'But I gave it my best shot.'

If Tiger Woods loses a game he accepts that gracefully, safe in the knowledge that he played his best. He gave of his best.

He may be going through a rough patch right now but I would be willing to bet, he'll be back.

If someone spoke

to you the way you

talk to yourself

you'd probably

slap him or her!

Some people would rather be right than happy

I remember an incident on the Oprah Winfrey show. Oprah is an exceptional person, who has done incredibly well against all the odds. She had a difficult childhood, but thankfully learned to read at the age of three. She has become a phenomenal success, but says frankly that she does not continue presenting her show just because she 'needs more shoes'. She continues because she knows she helps people and makes a difference. She definitely has a clear sense of purpose and self-awareness.

On one particular show Oprah had a guest called Iyanla Vanzant. Vanzant is an expert on the subject of self-esteem and has written several books on the subject, including *'In the Mean Time'*. She was on the show to talk to another, really successful, woman, who had an issue with all men. She'd had so many negative experiences that she believed all men were bad news. This particular lady I remember was very successful in most areas of her life. If she had done the 'Life Wheel' exercise in Figure 3.1, for example, I am sure she would have probably scored 10 on most of the spokes. This was a successful woman but she was not totally happy because she had no relationship. Now, her goal was to find the man of her dreams and have a family.

Iyanla asked her what she would expect from a date with a man:

'Not much,' she said, 'given what all men are like!'

'How do you behave, given this belief?' continued Iyanla.

'With caution and distance. I guess I am a bit closed, even cautious. I don't want to be hurt again!'

'What do your dates behave like if you're approaching them in this way?' asked Iyanla.

She laughed, realising right away what Iyanla was getting at.

'They are usually equally closed and cold,' she said.

'So, what results are you getting again?

'Exactly that. A cold and distant response.'

Now this woman was intelligent. Yet she needed this intervention to help realise that the results she was getting were a direct result of her beliefs about men.

When you behave in a certain way, as she had been doing, it was not surprising that she got that kind of negative response.

The interesting thing about this self-fulfilling prophecy is that it is based upon beliefs. The beliefs about men in this case drive her behaviour and her behaviour creates results. Results produce evidence and the evidence proves the belief to be right. It is a vicious cycle. Through her behaviour she maintained her belief.

Some people would rather be right than happy

The Belief Cycle

Please take a moment to consider if you recognise yourself in the 'Belief Cycle' shown in Figure 3.2.

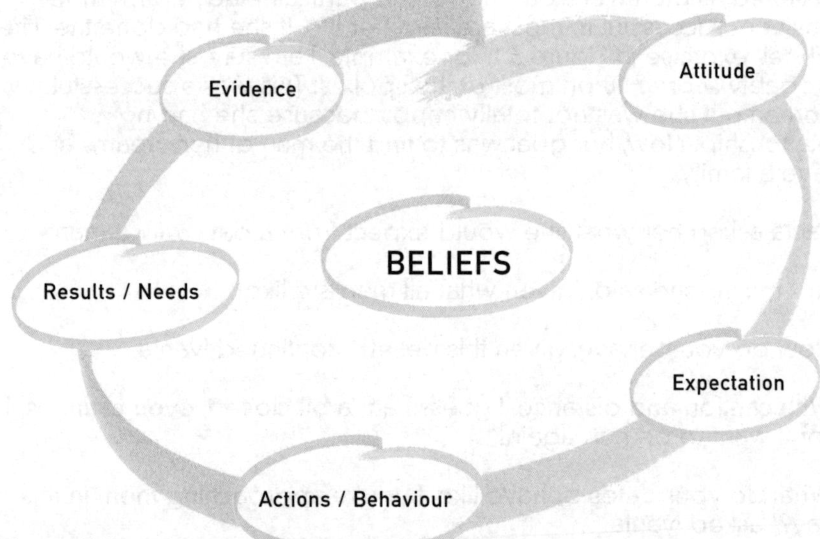

Figure 3.2

By the way it is interesting to notice that negative people like the lady in the example above, tend to surround themselves with like-minded people. It is almost as though they want external validation that their negative behaviour is acceptable, and who better to validate negative outcomes than negative people? For our lonely lady there may be nothing more therapeutic than a good old whine with friends. But at the end of it, she'll still be single.

Where your attention goes energy flows

So what's the High Performer's view on this kind of negative self-talk?

When you start looking for what you want rather than what you don't want you have a much greater chance of success. FOCUS ON THE DREAM NOT THE PROBLEM.

What do you believe?

Have you ever wondered where your beliefs come from?

Did you know that many of the beliefs you hold close to your heart were handed to you by your parents and relatives as a gift? You can choose to hold onto them or you can choose to let them go. Either way they are not part of you, they are not real, they are part of your *conditioning*.

Conditioning can be challenged and changed.

Set yourself up for success

When I was working in sales in the pharmaceutical industry, everyone on the sales team would see four customers a day. It was expected that you would see four. No-one seemed to realise that if they were to see more than four customers they had the potential to achieve more sales. Peer pressure is such that you slow your pace to match everyone else's. For this reason, everyone remained convinced that four was the 'gold standard'.

Why slow your pace to match everyone else's?

A High Performance Person doesn't slow his pace just to be one of the crowd. High Performance people push themselves to go the extra mile. They use appropriate language, such as I can and I choose to. They ask questions like what's possible? and what if? They talk kindly to themselves. They give themselves permission to expect and be the best at what they do.

When I got out in the field I saw between six and seven customers a day. I wanted to be Number One and I was lucky to have a manager who was supportive of my ambitions yet unrealistic about what was possible. My manager stretched me as much as he could. And guess what? In just three years I became the top salesman in the company.

Avoid negative self-talk

I remember when I was a young squash player and would have opponents who were quite a bit older than me. I would listen to them getting really cheesed off with themselves. They would shout and swear and get aggressive. I was always amused by this behaviour, and would watch my opponents slowly destroy themselves and their chances of winning.

Of course, this same kind of destructive, negative self-talk goes on in the business world as well. How many times have you said to yourself: 'I can't do this,' or, 'I'm not good enough'?
I bet you think of other negative phrases or beliefs that have crept into your regular work conversations. Such as:

- *This job is getting harder.*
- *It was much better before we had computers.*
- *Mondays are useless for getting to see anyone.*
- *The targets are always too high.*
- *They only see by appointment once a year if you are lucky.*
- *We just haven't got enough resources.*
- *It will never work, it didn't work before and it won't work now!*

I call this the Psychic Vampire syndrome, it de-energises you and it just is not helpful!

Remember that natural-born complainers can and will limit your success. Be very careful who you listen to and learn from.

Be careful who you mix with . . .

"The horse is here to stay, but the automobile is only a novelty- a fad."

These words were spoken by the president of Michigan Savings Bank, advising Henry Ford's lawyer not to invest in the Ford Motor Company

Be careful who you listen to . . .

Expect the best

The lady from the Oprah show is a great example of someone who created her own evidence and then set about proving herself right, time after time.

Next time you catch yourself believing something like that, ask yourself whether that belief is helping you to achieve your dream. Does it help or hinder? Does that belief move you closer to or further away from happiness? And where did the belief come from anyway? Was it a gift passed on to you by your family? Is it a belief you created yourself based on your own experience? Think about it.

What if?

It sounds too simple to be effective but it really can work . . .

As soon as you realise that one of your beliefs is holding you back you are more likely to open up to the possibility of new thinking. You can take on new beliefs.

One technique is simply to ask yourself a question. Just ask 'What if?'

- *What if I believed that success and happiness were not the privilege of the gifted few?*
- *What if anyone who applied simple principles and practices could achieve more out of life?*

Consider the two 'What If' questions, above. If you applied them to a current unhelpful belief how would that change things? Let's explore this further in the exercise below:

Existing belief

____

____

____

New belief

____

____

The benefits of adopting the new belief

If I adopted the new belief it would make me feel

I want to hold onto my old belief because

Look at what you have written for the above exercise. Think about it for a moment. Compare the difference between the outcomes of the old belief versus the new one.

I challenge you to try out this new belief for one month. Watch what happens. Notice how it opens up new possibilities.

High Performers challenge their 'hand me down' beliefs all the time.

I hope I don't get kicked

Set yourself up for failure and you are likely to fail.

I met Louise about two years ago on a High Performance Coaching Programme I was running. At the end of our first session she came up and told me her interesting story:

A few months earlier, Louise had taken her black belt grading for kick-boxing. She had dreamed of achieving this for many years and now her big moment had arrived. All Louise needed to do was her best. What happened to Louise that day is something that happens countless times in all manner of different situations the world over. The odd thing about Louise's story is that as she went into The Square, as they call it, the last thing that went through her mind was: 'I hope I don't get kicked'.

Sure enough, a few seconds into a full contact bout she was knocked out completely cold for a few seconds. This is not what you want to happen, of course.

Louise failed her exam.

As a result of this experience, Louise and I worked together on a few high performance processes during the two days of our programme. I made sure we included practising positive language patterns.

Several months later, three days before Louise's next grading, we met again and refocused on the outcome she wanted. I made Louise concentrate on the outcome her success would bring and to practise it. The way she did this was to picture herself winning and what it would give her - and to go through this again and again in her mind's eye. It was as if she were playing her own movie on constant replay.

When you want something badly, you need to visualise how having that thing will make you feel, where you will be and who you will be with when you have it. You need to think about how things will smell, what you will be wearing and every aspect of your life that could be affected by achieving your goal. Louise did this.

In fact, playing her new movie like this was very hard for Louise. Ever since that first and only black belt grading experience, she had not been able to get the bad movie, the negative story, out of her mind. She had been literally practising failure in her head.

Most of us already have all the gifts and talents we need inside us to achieve our dreams. The trouble is we don't acknowledge them.

I believe strongly that most people practise misery and failure in this way for much of their lives. Like most things, when you practise something enough you become quite good at it. Louise had become proficient at practising her own mini negative episode.

My role in this was simple. All I had to do was to keep reminding Louise of her brilliance, her skill and her ability. But I needed her to practise it for herself. I could not do that for her. For as long as Louise could identify herself with a successful, winning result, she would be sure to get her dream.

Louise had always trained hard. She was strong and fit and more than capable of being a black belt. Her only problem was that she did not believe it enough.

As the great golf coach Dr Bob Rotella, puts it . . . 'CONFIDENCE IS PLAYING WITH YOUR EYES.'

But there she was, playing her good movie in her head for just three days, after almost three months of playing the bad one.

Six months later, I received a letter from Louise. It read:

Dear Steve

I am absolutely chuffed. I passed my black belt.

Having failed before, I felt I needed something extra than physical ability to get me through the six hour examination and with your help I actually thought for the first time: 'I'm going to pass this'. After the exam I felt equally confident that I had passed too. This was very unusual for me.

I am completely sold on the positive thinking techniques you have shown me, which essentially gave me my confidence back. I could not have passed without them.

Louise

Most of us already have all the gifts and talents we need inside us, to achieve our dreams. The trouble is we don't acknowledge them.

Bad Movies

Have you ever been to a film and walked out before the end because the film was so bad? If you are like me you stay until the end only to find the film really was that bad!

Think of the last really awful film you saw at the cinema. When it came out on DVD or was on the Sky Box Office, did you make a point of buying or renting it again? Of course not. You would not be daft enough to watch a bad film a second time.

Well, think about your next big challenge - whether it will be in your professional or personal life. If the new experience has some similarity to an earlier experience, perhaps one where you have struggled, it is likely that you will find yourself thinking about your earlier negative experience.

I'll bet you play that internal video of the bad experience again and again in your head, don't you?

Think of the last difficult meeting you were in. Someone really upset you, so badly in fact you spent all weekend talking about the evil person who you now can't stand.

Now the meeting is coming round again. Which movie do you play?

Golfers and other sports people do this all the time. In fact they are really good at it. They play their last failure over and over again.

Why do we do this? We are all blessed with an imagination, so why don't we simply create ourselves a winning scene, an appealing movie, instead?

Bizarrely, the answer is that your brain can't tell the difference between what really happened and what you created in your imagination.

Tip
Be kind to yourself and stop playing bad movies now. Start creating yourself some empowering ones instead.

You don't need a wide plasma screen to do it. It costs nothing. I told you this book would be good. Now you get tips about free stuff too!

How Abby and I made our babies

Plan for success.

Even in the most difficult of circumstances you can still win through, as our story will illustrate:

Having a positive outlook is always more beneficial than having a negative one. But sometimes it can be a challenge to keep smiling.

In 1995 Abby and I lost twins at birth. 'Traumatised' does not even come close to describing our feelings.

I would be lying if I said there is some textbook coaching principle out there that helped us, and can help you to cope with a similar life-defining event. However, the way that Abby and I coped with our loss, and went on to cling to a positive outlook, is a good illustration of the expect the best theory in action.

We wanted Abby to be able to give birth to a healthy child and following our loss we were more determined than ever.

A few months after our trauma we had a meeting with a consultant, who shall remain nameless. His job was to guide us gently through our options. We went into that meeting feeling very delicate but cautiously optimistic.

We sat opposite him behind what seemed like a huge desk. He wore his white coat and his opening line I will never forget:

'Well, nothing looks good from where I'm sitting,' he began. His face remained fixed and emotionless

'The way I see it you have three options,' he continued.

'Either you can do nothing at all. This is not a good option, but it is still an option.'

By this time Abby was in tears and I only just held on. Today was a grey day, literally. Abby and I sat there in silence.

'Or you can take a fertility drug which carries a risk of cancer.' Option two didn't sound too good either, but at least we had one more option to go.

'Or you can have an operation that has a 15 per cent chance of leaving you sterilised.'

When you want something really badly nothing will stop you putting every ounce of energy into it.

'Is that it?' I said incredulously.

'Well, I did say that nothing looks good,' replied the doctor.

We left the consultation room feeling helpless. I remember that Abby phoned her mum to tell her the news. Gulping back tears, Abby told her that it looked like we would never have children.

We were gutted and spent many days almost in a daze. Hopeless didn't even come close to describing our feelings. We were still grieving the loss of our babies and rational thought was neither easy nor expected.

But our hopelessness turned into bloody determination and passion. When you want something really badly nothing will stop you putting every ounce of energy into it. We had determination and passion in abundance.

When you want something really badly nothing will stop you putting every ounce of energy into it.

A few weeks later we went back to see the same doctor. This time we were ready.

- We had done our research.
- We had sought out friends with similar EXPERIENCES.
- We'd been on the Internet.
- We read articles, books, ANYTHING RELEVANT WE COULD GET OUR HANDS ON.
- We knew all our options.

We had prepared ourselves for each possible outcome. We had carefully considered our most optimistic, our good and our minimum outcomes. In other words, we had already decided what was the least we would accept, the best we could expect and something in between. We had what we call a WELL-FORMED OUTCOME.

We were ready.

This time, sitting in the same consultation room with the same doctor, we listened once more to the same choices that we had on offer. But this time we challenged him. Abby and I had found out about a process called *follicular tracking*, where the hospital monitors the ovaries every day until they are sure an egg is ready - and then you go home and attempt to conceive. DIY as it's called!

We asked the doctor about this process. He did not seem keen. He told us that it would be very time consuming for us and that we would have to go to the hospital daily for unlimited weeks. Each trip to the hospital meant a 60 mile round trip.

'That's OK,' we said.

This time our meeting with the consultant had a completely different atmosphere. We had a whole new attitude. We took control. Even in the face of the forces of nature we forged ahead. We would not be beaten by something as trivial and manageable as a 60 mile journey.

We had influenced a significant shift in the outcome. We agreed a number of new options that blatantly had been kept from us due to time or money. Either way we were making progress.

Next we asked for a second opinion and were referred to a different consultant, Mr Goswami. Mr Goswami read through Abby's notes carefully, which, by the way, we provided ourselves as we had guessed that the other consultant would not provide the vital medical history needed.

We were thorough and proactive. We left nothing to chance.

He read every word of Abby's hand written notes.

He looked up and met our eyes.

'This looks really good for you,' he said. Then he took a blank sheet of paper and I remember he wrote PLAN in the top corner.' And then he smiled.

'This is what we need to do . . .' he began.

Amazing, wasn't it, that the same patients with the same history could see a different doctor and get a completely different reaction?

Mr Goswami planned our treatment and within 15 months of meeting him Christopher was born weighing nine pounds and 13 ounces. He is now nine years old.

Two years later Anna was born naturally. And we are now a very happy family of four.

Having well-formed outcomes is all about BEING CLEAR ABOUT WHAT YOU WANT.

Achieving what you want means you need to pursue your dreams with passion and determination. Making your dreams come true requires that you seek advice from the right people. And of course, we also learned to never give in.

But maybe there is another lesson there too? You may have to do a lot of things on your own, but you cannot do the whole job alone, without the support, advice and encouragement of other people.

You have to do it by yourself but you cannot do it alone

We had learned a really powerful lesson.

Many times when I work with top sports people they are cautious about expecting the very best. They may not want to aim for first place just in case they fail. The theory seems to be that if they don't expect to win then losing is going to be more palatable, more acceptable.

This is a cop out and it doesn't work.

When Abby got pregnant with Christopher she was really really ill. Hyper emesis is a condition of constant vomiting during pregnancy. It is stressful, draining, and depressing. Having lost twins in a previous pregnancy we were both very fearful. We were kind of expecting that we might end up suffering again.

Abby was admitted to hospital and given fluids via a drip and I just watched every day as she slowly fell away inside herself.

She could barely communicate.

Out of desperation I called Mr Goswami and asked him to come in and see Abby. Maybe he could help?

I remember the day like it was yesterday.

He asked me to leave and went in to find Abby lying flat and deflated. Almost lifeless. She was about 12 weeks pregnant and had lost a significant amount of weight. She was pale and drawn. After 20 minutes Goswami came out.

'You can go in now,' he said.

As I entered I found Abby sitting up, still very weak but sitting up and smiling. Now I knew Goswami was good, but this was unbelievable. What had he done?

Abby looked at me and said, 'Honey, we're going to have a baby. We need to start to get ready.'

Until that point we had decided not to buy anything. We had decided that it was going to be too painful to prepare a nursery, buy clothes and to celebrate the pregnancy. So we just expected the worst.

Our theory was that if we expected this pregnancy to fail then we would in some way be less affected, less sad, if it did.

The truth is that whether we expected success or failure another loss would be devastating either way. So we may as well enjoy the journey.

Mr Goswami reminded us to enjoy the experience. He told me that we were going to have a baby and to worry less.

How many times do you miss out on the joys of life, the great experiences because you are fearful of failure?

The point is that if you simply expect the best then more often than not the BEST or something EVEN BETTER will turn up!

A word on fear

In 1987 Susan Jeffers wrote an outstanding book called '*Feel the Fear and do it Anyway*', in which she talks about fear as a good thing. She writes:

'The presence of fear is a sign that you are growing and accepting life's challenges.' – Susan Jeffers.

Expect the best

Think about it. If 90% of what we worry about never happens why not expect the best instead? You will still feel bloody awful if it doesn't work out but you will have trained yourself to react in a more constructive way. Instead of saying 'That's terrible' you might say, 'What I have learned is . . . or 'What's next, then?'

Fear is inevitable but all the best performers fail at some point. Some fail many times over. High Performers embrace failure and fear as part of the process.

Here's a question that Nigel Risner asked me many years ago and it really makes you think.

'What would you do if you ABSOLUTELY KNEW YOU COULD NOT FAIL?'

What stops you going for what you want?

Promise me that you will start expecting the best right now.

Most of us ALREADY HAVE THE GIFTS AND TALENTS WE NEED inside us, to achieve our dreams. The trouble is we don't acknowledge them.

You have to do it by yourself but you cannot do it alone.

se what yo[u]
at you eat and you ch[oose]
ices. So here's the thing. This bo[ok]
ou unless you categorically agree with bot[h]
ou don't agree now and know that you never will, then
own and go off and do something else... Still here? Excellent! Th
set of the few - the High Performance mindset that is guaranteed to set you
ent, achievement and happiness. It's up to you What's in it for you? This book will
that have been proven to make a difference in individual and team performance. And becau
on't find High Performance natural we have to be disciplined to apply what we learn and take
et something else straight right up front. If you want an easy ride to a better richer life STOP RE
ok NOW and accept that what you have is what you will probably end up with . . . . The ideas h
in theory but clearly if they were all so easy to implement everyone would be doing them, w
d they're not. All HIGH PERFORMING, successful PEOPLE that I have met or read about, WORK
LLY REALLY HARD. This stuff is not quick fix. PMA Mohammed Ali was one of the world's great
n. He was possibly the definitive world champion boxer. Many remember Ali as cocky, even a
istical. They thought he was a cheeky young man who talked a good game. In a recent docum
coach recently said that the sportsman was the hardest working boxer he had ever met BOTH
THE RING. He trained harder, practised more and of course had INCREDIBLE self-belief. Ali ha
just PMA, which stands for Positive Mental Attitude, by the way. Do you think PMA is a good th
you do. So do [illegible] let's be honest, here. Having a PMA does not guarantee success. For exa
ided to run in the [illegible] sprint at the Olympics right now, with no specific training, it would not
all the PMA in the w[orld] [illegible] still be unlikely to win. But with PMA you would probably
loser. PMA is part of the deal [illegible] means the answer to your problems. It's up to y
chief executive of your life. That mea[ns] you [ch]oose what you do, who you spen[d]
th. what you eat and you choose the consequences of those choices. It's up to y
ance People make a habit of doing the things that unsuccessful people find uncomfortable. O
ave met thousands of amazing people with AWESOME natural talent. Yet few of them fulfil thei
many never even recognise their gifts. They simply go unused. In fact, most people appear to
would call NEAR LIFE EXPERIENCES. They are always about to make the big change, but some
busy. They think they will get round to doing it NOW. Hardly anyone ever says 'I'll start my
orrow', or 'I'll give up smoking next week,' they are not [illegible] If it's worth doing it's wor
WIN Disease (I Want It Now) You know, this is not rocket science. The things that make a real di
life are remarkably [illegible] understand and they lie well within your grasp right now. But ther
Most of us are 'bone i[dle]'. Have you noticed how many people seem to want an easy rout
d financial freedom? They will happily buy a product called Slim Quick because they are con
solve their weight problems, yet deep down they know that slimming is a combination of de
upport, discipline, drive and motivation. It takes time to reach a target weight, to adjust a met
ge a lifestyle. And even though they know that all this EFFORT AND HARD WORK will probably
ovascular risks and give them more energy for a longer life, they still buy Slim Quick. Come o
t daft, just lazy!!! It's up to you High Performance People make a habit of doing the
successful people find uncomfortable. It's up to you 80/20 I expect you will have hea
20 theory beforeIn simple terms it says that 80% of results, inventions or whatever com
of the population. This law holds true in every environment I have encountered through my w
re. When I run my seminars, after the students have had three days learning motivational and
s on performance, I ask the following question: Based on Pareto's law I know that only 20% of
do anything different when you leave this seminar. Show me by raising your hand if you will b
Guess what? Every hand goes up. Yet I know that the law will hold true. 80% will do nothing
ll do diddlysquat. Every day, thousands of books like this one are bought (though not read n
e listen to CDs and attend seminars all the time, yet very few of them actually do anything dif
Why should this be? As I said earlier, WE CRAVE FOR SOMETHING MORE. But somehow we
ered to go and get it. It's somehow easier to settle for what we have and live a NEAR LIFE exp
this: You will probably live for 80 years based upon current medical developments. If you NE
u really want for the rest of your life how will you feel? If the Pareto Principle is true then you w
an [eff]ort if you want to be in that 20%. A bit of effort is all it takes. And you may spend the res
enj[oyin]g even more happiness and fulfilment, which you deserve by the way. It's up to you M
idle' It's up to you I was recently on holiday in France and spent some time with the Ma
[illegible] Peter was only 21 but was easily the most professional holiday company repres
[de]veloped a problem with the brakes and Peter had willingly gone the ex
himself to organise a swift service at a good price. On the wa
first joined his company when he had been just 18 y
[illegible] suit so he would look his best (he s
[illegible] prepared a file of his achievem
[illegible] questions and an
[illegible] waited

SIXTY SECOND SUMMARY

- *Self awareness is the first step in moving forward and fulfilling potential..*
- *Some people set themselves up to fail. A phenomenon known as Self Handicapping.*
- *Expecting the best means focusing on what you want and training your inner voice to support you.*
- *Beware of the bad movies you are playing.*
- *Beliefs are hand-me-downs and they can be changed.*
- *Expecting failure will not make failing any easier to accept. So you might as well enjoy the journey.*
- *Fear is a natural emotion hat all high performers experience. It is a sign that you are growing.*

Headstart

CHAPTER 4

MOTIVATIONAL FUEL

We are not motivated by what we already have.

Why you should read this chapter:

- Principally because **high performers set goals**.
- So you will **learn practical tips** on setting effective goals and how to take action on them.
- So you will also learn how important it is to set **well structured goals** so that they become motivational and achievable.
- Because many **people don't follow through on a goal** no matter how much they appear to want it.
- Because you need to **work to your strengths** to maximise your potential.
- Because you will learn to **make the most of what you've got**.

No book on personal performance would be complete without a few words about goals and how to set and achieve them.

Here are some practical thoughts and ideas to help you:

What do you need?

In 1954 Abraham Maslow wrote about motivation. He told us about what he named the 'Hierarchy of Needs'. He said that human needs had three levels. The most basic level of need comprises air, food and water. The next level up comprises, safety, love and self-esteem. The topmost level was for what he called self-actualisation.

In simple terms, what this boils down to is the fact that:

We are not motivated by what we already have

So, if you have water, food and a roof over your head then acquiring these things is not likely to motivate you to do something different. You take them for granted. If you do not have these things then you are VERY motivated to obtain them.

However, when these basic needs are provided for and we no longer have to worry about them then we look to achieve something more. We look for safety, love and self-esteem.

Goals keep us motivated. Effective goals are aligned to your purpose.

And then, similarly, when those things are within our grasp we then yearn for the next level, that of self-actualisation, or, what you might like to call the Desire to Achieve, to Learn and to Make a Difference. A HUMAN DESIRE TO FULFILL OUR POTENTIAL, TO STRETCH AND TO GROW

Goals keep us motivated
Effective goals are aligned to your purpose

In Chapter Two, 'Know What You Want', you wrote yourself a Success Statement that made sense to you. Now it is time for you to prepare yourself an Action Plan or Life Plan to help you to achieve the kind of success you crave. An Action Plan will start you heading in the right direction.

Whenever you go for a job interview, you are asked about where you see yourself in one, three, five or even ten years' time. We know that we are expected to have long term, medium term and short term goals, but some of us just simply do not know where we want to be, or what we want to have achieved in 25 years' time. I know I don't. You might only know where you want to go on holiday next summer and that you would like to spend more time with your family.

People are more short term these days. Things change so quickly. We can no longer rely on having a job, or a client or a career for life.

In Colin Rose's book '*Accelerated Learning in the 21st Century*', Rose writes about the changing world and the way that we can no longer ask our children what they want to do when they grow up. More accurately we might ask, what they want to do first!!

Typically, our own parents had one career, or just one significant job change. We expect our children to have seven or eight different careers and countless jobs. But in spite of this trend we are more in control than we think. We still need to be in the habit of setting goals and achieving them. So we set short term goals, like a target weight perhaps or a luxury holiday or a promotion or earnings goal. We set ourselves relationship goals too. You see, we still set goals.

Goals drive and motivate us, especially when they allow us to use our strengths. They keep us on track. They give us a sense of direction. I have found with many youngsters who have a keen interest in a sport or activity, goal setting keeps their attention and focus.

Think back to the 'My Favourite Things' and 'Successes' exercises in Chapter Two. Look at your talents and strengths again. If you want to be motivated to achieve your goals you may want to make more use of them.

One at a time, please

Think about the England rugby team. They achieved the ultimate status in sport and became world champions. Four years' work culminated in their amazing performance in Australia in 2003.

In a recent interview the team members reflected on their experience. Interestingly, they said that lifting that trophy was awesome, and one that they will never forget. A goal achieved. Then they spoke of being struck with the sudden thought: 'What the hell do we do now?'

Martin Johnson (England captain at the time) hadn't actually made his mind up to retire at that moment. He most certainly didn't know what he was going to do next.

The goal of the England rugby team was to become world champions. It was an all-consuming goal. It motivated 30 young athletes to a once in a lifetime achievement. The goal served its purpose and then they moved on. It was not until they had reached their goal that they could think beyond it.

You see, you don't have to have your life mapped out step by step. But you do need goals. You need them to get you focused, motivated and feeling alive. I was privileged to meet Cathy O'Dowd, the first woman to conquer Everest from both north and south sides. She described her emotional journey and how they would feel both positive and drained as each stage of the climb was achieved. There were times when she felt so tired that giving in seemed the only option. But the next goal kept her focused (that, of course, and the support of her team).

Her next goal could be something as simple as the distance they would walk, reaching a certain marker or an altitude. The goals kept them focused and kept them moving onward and upward. Sometimes the goal was to be in a shelter, to ensure survival. When you need something in order to survive, as Maslow explains, that'll get you motivated!

Jamie Clarke from Canada is also an adventurer and after three attempts he reached the summit of Everest. He was very clear that sometimes you have to shift your goal as your original aim may no longer be appropriate. On one of their failed attempts, they were less than 100 yards from the big goal, the summit, but recognised that someone would have probably died had they gone for it. The goal shifted, instead, to survival. In achieving this goal they forfeited the original goal, but their lives depended on it.

Goals are our motivational fuel

Take a moment now to think about goals you have set for yourself during your life.

List some of your goals here:

____

____

How did each goal make you feel?

____

____

How did attempting each goal make you behave?

____

____

Did attempting each goal make you feel driven?

____

____

Did attempting each goal give you more energy?

____

____

Goals only work when you set them up right, so that they motivate you. This is the only way you can have a fighting chance of achieving them.

Make time for happiness now.

ose what y
hat you eat and you
hoices. So here's the thing. This
you unless you categorically agree with
you don't agree now and know that you never will,
down and go off and do something else... Still here? Excellent.
dset of the few - the High Performance mindset that is guaranteed to set yo
ment, achievement and happiness. **It's up to you** What's in it for you? This book will
as that have been proven to make a difference in individual and team performance. And beca
don't find High Performance natural we have to be disciplined to apply what we learn and tak
get something else straight right up front. If you want an easy ride to a better richer life STOP
ook NOW and accept that what you have is what you will probably end up with . . . The ideas
le in theory but clearly if they were all so easy to implement everyone would be doing them,
nd they're not. All HIGH PERFORMING, successful PEOPLE that I have met or read about, WOR
ALLY REALLY HARD. This stuff is not quick fix. PMA Mohammed Ali was one of the world's grea
en. He was possibly the definitive world champion boxer. Many remember Ali as cocky, even
otistical. They thought he was a cheeky young man who talked a good game. In a recent docu
s coach recently said that the sportsman was the hardest working boxer he had ever met BOT
OF THE RING. He trained harder, practised more and of course had INCREDIBLE self-belief. Ali h
n just PMA, which stands for Positive Mental Attitude, by the way. Do you think PMA is a good
e you do. So do I. But let's be honest, here. Having a PMA does not guarantee success. For ex
ecided to run in the 100m sprint at the Olympics right now, with no specific training, it would no
d all the PMA in the world, you would still be unlikely to win. But with PMA you would probab
y loser. PMA is part of the deal but it is by no means the answer to your problems. **It's up to**
he chief executive [illegible] **ur life. That means you choose what you do, who you spe**
vith, what you eat [illegible] **the consequences of those choices. It's up to**
mance People make a habit of [illegible] things that unsuccessful people find uncomfortable.
have met thousands of amazing people with [illegible] ent. Yet few of them fulfil th
many never even recognise their gifts. They simply [illegible] ed. [illegible] most people appear t
I would call NEAR [illegible] FE EXPERIENCES. They are always about to make [illegible] big change, but som
o busy. They think [illegible] round to doing it TOMORROW. If anyone ever says 'I'll start m
morrow', or 'I'll give up [illegible] k,' they are not committed. If it's worth doing it's wo
IWIN Disease (I Want It Now) You know [illegible] ket science. The things that make a real
ur life are remarkably easy to understand and [illegible] ell within your grasp right now. But th
h: Most of us are 'bone idle' Have you noticed how many [illegible] to want an easy rou
nd financial freedom? They will happily buy a product called Slim Quick because they are co
esolve their weight problems, yet deep down they know that slimming is a combination of d
support, discipline, drive and motivation. It takes time to reach a target weight, to adjust a me
ge a lifestyle. And even though they know that all this EFFORT AND HARD WORK will probab
diovascular risks and give them more energy for a longer life, they still buy Slim Quick. Come
n't daft, just lazy!!! **It's up to you High Performance People make a habit of doing th**
nsuccessful people find uncomfortable It's up to you 80/20 I expect you will have he
0/20 theory beforeIn simple terms it says that 80% of profits, results, inventions or whatever co
% of the population. This law holds true in every environment I have encountered through my
ure. When I run my seminars, after the students have had three days learning motivational an
as on performance, I ask the following question: Based on Pareto's law I know that only 20%
do anything different when you leave this seminar. Show me by raising your hand if you will
. Guess what? Every hand goes up. Yet I know that the law will hold true. 80% will do nothing
vill do diddlysquat. Every day, thousands of books like this one are bought (though not read
ple listen to CDs and attend seminars all the time, yet very few of them actually do anything
t. Why should this be? As I said earlier, WE CRAVE FOR SOMETHING MORE. But somehow we
ered to go and get it. It's somehow easier to settle for what we have and live a NEAR LIFE ex
r this: You will probably live for 80 years based upon current medical developments. If you N
ou really want for the rest of your life how will you feel? If the Pareto Principle is true then you
e a[illegible]ort if you want to be in that 20%. A bit of effort is all it takes. And you may spend the re
enj[illegible]g even more happiness and fulfilment, which you deserve by the way. It's up to you
e idle' **It's up to you** I was recently on holiday in France and spent some time with the M
any. Peter was only 21 but was easily the most professional holiday company repre
developed a problem with the brakes and Peter had willingly gone the
himself to organise a swift service at a good price. On the w
first joined his company when he had been just 18
posh suit so he would look his best (he
prepared a file of his achieve
the questions and a
he waite

Celebrate the little things

People who are more motivated, upbeat and optimistic are generally the same people who commit to short, medium or long term goals. They promise themselves that they will have achieved certain things by the end of the month, the week or the year - and then they give themselves a reward of some kind as each small step is achieved. Maybe the reward will be a bottle of wine at the end of the week, or a day off?

I remember when I set up Headstart I promised my family a trip to Disneyland in Florida if I made a six figure income in the first year. We had a great trip! That personal goal set by me and for me drove me towards a very successful year.

Robert Holden, author of several books on happiness including '*Laughter is the Best Medicine*' talks of 'happiness now'. He writes that too many people are so busily searching for 'something else' that they forget to make time for any happiness now.

So be ready to celebrate your small achievements along the way.

Make time for happiness now

Let it GROW

In the 70's Graham Alexander created what was to become one of the definitive coaching models. It has been used by coaches and organisations ever since.

The model is well known and can help you to set and create a plan towards achieving your goals. It is really simple to understand and implement. Strangely however, it is often used ineffectively or not used at all.

The model looks like this:

G **Goal**

R **Reality**

O **Options**

W **What now?**

Goals

Ask yourself what you want to do or be, and what your short term goals are. Maybe you don't want to be the best in the world at what you do - but you might want to be the best in your county or town, the best in your club, or the best in your office. Or simply strive to improve at some level. Athletes often have Personal Bests (PBs).

Write here some of your short term goals:

____

____

____

Once you know what you want to be, ask yourself why you want that. Is it because you want the wealth, the lifestyle or the fame that goes with it? The why question is not built into GROW but there is high value in thinking about your motivation. When you have a goal, you have a hope of achieving it only if you have a passion, or a reason, for wanting what it can give you.

Kriss Akabusi wanted to be a 400 metre hurdle champion because he wanted the recognition that went with it. As a rule, sportsmen are pretty clear about their goals. They set personal goals such as a personal best time, or a distance to run. They call these goals 'performance goals'. They also have a clear outcome goal to work towards. This is a major overriding goal that motivates them through training and interim events. For serious athletes this is usually Olympics.

Other people may not know so clearly what they want - but half the battle is ensuring that you have a passion for achieving each of your goals because you truly desire the effect of that achievement.

Note your reasons for wanting to achieve your goals here:

____

____

____

____

A really good WHY can make the difference between achieving or not!

Remember Louise's story? Visualisation is a big part of goal setting.

Try this now.

Think of one really big goal you want to go for. It might be writing a book, getting your handicap down or getting promoted for example.

Write that goal down here:

____

____

You can do the next part of the exercise with someone you trust. But for now, you can write down your response. Later you can do this out loud:

Write here the words you would use to your friend, that describe how you FELT once you achieved that goal. Describe it in detail, using all of your senses. If your goal was writing a book, then describe the book jacket, how heavy it was, whether it was hard back or softback, how much it cost, which bookshops sold it. Say what it was about and what the reviewers said. How did it feel when you held it in your hand for the first time? Go mad. I've given you plenty of space so you can write about how it FELT when you achieved your goal:

____

____

____

____

____

____

____

____

Well now you are getting closer to a real goal. Once you begin to get excited about a goal you can almost taste it. Then you know it's real and it's possible.

Make it happen

I remember when I took squash up at 15 I was determined to become county champion by the time I was 16.

The night before the final I lay in bed playing every shot in my head. I was so into the experience that I actually found myself getting out of breath. I was so ready the next day because I had played this match over and over.

I WON 3 LOVE (that's good by the way) and the guy I beat I had never beaten before that day. Why?

- I had trained every day
- I had practised every day
- I had hooked up with the best player in the area as a training partner

In other words I had done the hard physical stuff but the icing on the cake was, in part, due to powerful visualisation.

By the way, I hadn't given a moment's thought to my next goal, the one that would come after I became county champion. All I wanted was the county under 19's title. Nevertheless, once I achieved my goal, my next one was to hold onto the title. I certainly had no idea that, 24 years later, I would end up being a professional speaker and high performance specialist.

Reality

Before you can get cracking on achieving your goals, you have to ask yourself where you are right now on your journey. You also need to make sure you have all the facts. You have to get real as Dr Phil McGraw, Oprah Winfrey's TV relationship expert, would say.

You may not expect, honestly, to become the best cook in the world - but could you aim to be the best in your class? If so, then where are you now? Are you fairly average in a class of 20, or are you somewhere near the top?

Control the controllables

You may want to be the best golfer in the world and right now you are 500th in the world. Ask yourself what you can control that would help you achieve that goal. You could train every day.

A really good WHY can make the difference between achieving or not!

That is controllable. You could hire a coach to help improve your game.

That is controllable. You could play in ten new tournaments over the next year. That is controllable. You can invest in the best clubs and equipment . . . You get the idea.

Now ask yourself: What is not controllable?
The weather, the state of the course, the competitors' performance, perhaps? They are not controllable. So do not put your energy and attention into thinking about things you cannot control.

Consider this: If you are feeling a bit tired you might be tempted to eat a Mars bar.

When you eat a chocolate bar, you will get a sugar surge, a temporary burst of energy from the snack. Shortly afterwards you will get a post-prandial dip as the sugar levels in your blood fall and then, in fact, you end up feeling worse than you did before you ate the chocolate! Have you noticed that?

In fact, you would feel better off having a drink of water, rather than the chocolate.

What you eat is controllable. What is not controllable is the way the chocolate bar, or the water, makes you feel as a result.

Golfers cannot control the weather. They say that proactive people take their sunshine with them. So, you might not be able to control the weather - but you can control how the rain makes you feel.

High Performance People do not blame external circumstances, such as the weather, for how they perform.

Gary Player is one of the greatest golfers ever to play the game. He had just arrived at a golf tournament and was practising on particularly fast greens. He was heard to say, 'I always putt my best on fast greens.'

A week later, he was on a different course preparing on the slowest greens of the season. When asked how he felt he said, 'Well you know I always putt my best on slow greens'.

Bryan Beeson, ex British champion and world top ten squash player was my Number One influence in my approach to the game. He would hear me talking a good game and very quickly bring me back down to size.

'Shut up and play squash.' Beeson would say. Let your racket do the talking.

Understanding your reality is essential before you start making decisions about goal achievement.

In my experience, we are not particularly good at self-awareness. What I mean is we often focus on our weaknesses and short falls. We do not naturally acknowledge how good we are at something and constantly compare ourselves to others. It can therefore be difficult for us to evaluate our own reality. So you might do well to get support from a coach or trusted friend.

Feedback, in this instance, is a vital part of the process. This is where coaching makes the biggest difference. I'll talk more about feedback in the next chapter.

This kind of intervention will serve to remind you of your strengths, talents and your natural brilliance. All things that you probably don't think about, or focus on, enough. Remember we talked about brilliance in Chapter Three.

Write down here your own reality statement, based on what you know, or what people can tell you about where you are now in relation to the goal you selected earlier:

____

____

____

____

____

____

____

____

____

____

Options

The next thing to do is consider which of the options available to you will help you achieve your goals. Your options are all the things you could do in order to achieve your goal. All the different ways you could get what you want. In a way we are back to talking about What If!

Think of as many options as you can. Don't judge them.

It is important to be optimistic and open-minded. You have to give every option or every idea a chance to be considered.

> *Tip*
> *Don't share your creative ideas with a Psychic Vampire (negative person). They will very quickly block your creativity and drain your energy.*

Scenario plan

Write down all the options you have open to you right now in order to achieve the goal you selected earlier:

____

____

____

____

What now?

So, you have set your goals, done a reality check, and considered the options you have available to you. Now you just need to decide what to do next. This is about choosing options and taking action.

Sounds simple, but is it? Well it's the one part of the plan that is most likely not to happen because as I said right at the start of this book, most people are drawn to the path of least resistance. The thinking and planning bit is actually quite easy but the thought of taking action, well that's going to take effort. It might even be a little uncomfortable.

Good things do not come to those who wait idly on their backsides hoping that some freak of good fortune will turn their lives around.

I am 42 years old as I write this book and I can safely say that NOTHING I have ever achieved or acquired that has been of any real significant value to me has been handed to me for free. I have had to go out and work extremely hard, make loads of mistakes, fail and then eventually win through.

Good things do not come to those who wait idly on their backsides hoping that some freak of good fortune will turn their lives around.

Try this. Think of something you want or need that carries a really high value to you, like a career change, to be physically fitter or to become financially independent.

Now do nothing different. Mix with the same people you always have, think the same thoughts, keep the same negative inner voice chatting away at you, keep watching the same amount of television and eating the wrong food. Go on; just do what you've always done.

Call me in five years time and tell me how your dreams are coming along. If you have achieved what you wanted then go out and buy a lottery ticket because believe me you are one lucky human being.

I'm not joking.

Generally speaking, lasting, wholesome, contentment, success and happiness just do not turn up out of the blue. It really does take effort.

'If you do what you've always done, you'll get what you've always got.' – Abraham Maslow

'If you do what

you've always done,

you'll get what

you've always got.'

- Abraham Maslow

So, write here what you are going to do NOW to achieve your goal:

____

____

____

____

____

____

Welcome to the world of High Performance!

Why we fail

As I mentioned earlier, often the reason why most of us don't take action is FEAR.

Fear of failure or fear that what we hope to achieve might not work. Fear that we may lose what we already have. In fact in researching this book I spoke with many people who are frustrated in their jobs or with their lives generally and want more. They have a dream or the spark of an idea that excites them and could lead to a better life but they are really scared that if they go for it and it doesn't work then they've given up everything. They have a lot to lose.

I'm sure you know the story. It goes something like this . . .

> ***'I have a mortgage and a family to support I can't just pack everything in to train as a psychologist. I need my income. I just have to accept it, I took a wrong turn 20 years ago and I have to live with it. I'll just have to go on having a NEAR LIFE experience.'***

Sound familiar? While I relate to this situation, I do not subscribe to it.

The truth is that fears like these are common and natural. But what good will it do if I simply say, 'Oh well, if you're scared, you're scared.'

You need some practical advice to get you moving. It is my job to make things happen.

In Chapter Six, 'Create a Dream Team', we will look more deeply into ways to make things happen, but for now, to round off this chapter, here is a simple check list that high performance people use to take action and often realise a goal:

Bringing goals to life

1.Clarify Your Goal
Define your goal. Be clear of what it is and what it means to you. Be clear why going for your goal is worth the bother. Ensure you are motivated to achieve it.

2. Write it down
Evidence suggests that people who write down a goal are more likely to achieve it. Be as detailed as possible when you write yours down.

The great golf coach, Nick Mitchell was told as a young golfer to write his acceptance speech before taking part in an event so he was prepared for success. His game improved immediately even though his coach hadn't even given him a lesson.

3. Practise Success
Visualise it, feel it, explore it as though it is happening or has happened. Allow yourself to get excited about it.

Take Nick's idea, above, and write down the experience of your goal being achieved. Use your imagination, get carried away. Write in the past tense and use descriptive words to give life and colour. If you do this well you should actually feel your heart race, and genuinely get excited.

4. Share it
Share your goal with a supporter, someone you trust. Maybe a coach or mentor? There is no better motivator than getting support (and sometimes being nagged by) someone who has a vested interest in seeing you succeed.

Think about Weight Watchers' clubs. This dieting method often works because it provides a support network for members. You are accountable to others and not just yourself. You even get applauded if you reach your target weight! Discover the benefits of sharing your goal with other people who recognise you can't reach your target weight in one session! Which leads me to a vital step in action planning phase:

5. Make it bite size

Create smaller, short term goals. What would be a good first step? It may be as simple as get up one hour earlier to read a book on your subject. What often holds people back is the sheer scale of the goals they have set themselves.

In my experience from both a personal perspective and through my friends and clients who ultimately achieve their dreams, people are good at breaking a big goal into smaller, manageable steps. Each step being achievable in terms of time, energy, support and so on. As this is the commitment stage, you need to ensure you can commit.

A few years ago I read a great book called 'How to Think Like a Millionaire', which featured 10 very famous people including Ray Croc of McDonald's, Thomas Watson of IBM, Steven Spielberg and so on. After I read that book one tip stood out in my mind above all.

That in order to create your new life you should get up one hour earlier every day and dedicate it to your life goal. This means that every week you have seven hours, which adds up to at least 28 hours a month and 364 hours in a year. That means that in one year you could spend the equivalent of 52 DAYS on your goal.

Do you think that 52 days dedicated to your goals and dreams would make a difference?

This idea is so simple and achievable, but again most people don't do this simple thing because, you guessed it - it's too hard. It's easier to moan that there are simply not enough hours in the day.

6. Commit

In order to achieve your goal you need to commit to several things. You need to commit to:

Taking the first step.

Involving your support team along the way so they will hold you accountable.

Making your commitment both timed and measurable. This means your achievement will be done by a certain date and can be measured.

Writing down how you will recognise that you have achieved your goal.

How often you want your support team to chase you up and check on your progress.

Recognising the consequences of not achieving your goal and, more importantly, the benefits of success.

How you will reward yourself when you achieve your goal.

Be careful of deadlines

In December 1999 I was getting more and more excited about the possibility of setting up my own company. I met with one of my mentors, Nigel Risner, for breakfast near Heathrow airport (I think I paid!) to share my dream. I told him I had even decided that June 30th 2000, six months from that date was the date I would GO FOR IT!

Nigel was so supportive of me and my idea that day but I remember his advice very clearly.

'Don't hold yourself to the timescale you have set, it might work but it might also just put you under unnecessary stress and pressure Remember you have Abby and the family to consider too,' he said.

His words gave me permission to feel more relaxed about the BIG DAY. In fact it actually arrived almost 18 months later, a year beyond my original date. I will explain more about this and how it happened in Chapter Seven.

Don't get me wrong, deadlines and timescales are certainly valuable. Imagine you're an athlete training for the Olympics, for example. Obviously you can't push back the event just because you're not quite ready! Sometimes deadlines are essential to get you focused and can work very well indeed for some of your Bite Size Chunks (such as writing the first chapter of your book by the end of the month, for example). Deadlines keep you on track. But if you have followed the steps outlined here and you are motivated and passionate you will get there in the end. And when the time is right to take the BIG LEAP you will know. Trust me you will know.

SIXTY SECOND SUMMARY

- *Goals are motivational when they are constructed well.*
- *You don't necessarily need to have life long goals, short term goals can energise and inspire you if they have meaning.*
- *A coach will help you to clarify your goals, define the first steps and hold you accountable.*
- *Most people who achieve their desired results almost always get support.*
- *Even the most motivated self-starters need to break their goals down into bite size pieces.*
- *Remember to celebrate small achievements along the way.*
- *Work to your strengths as this will maximise your chances of success.*

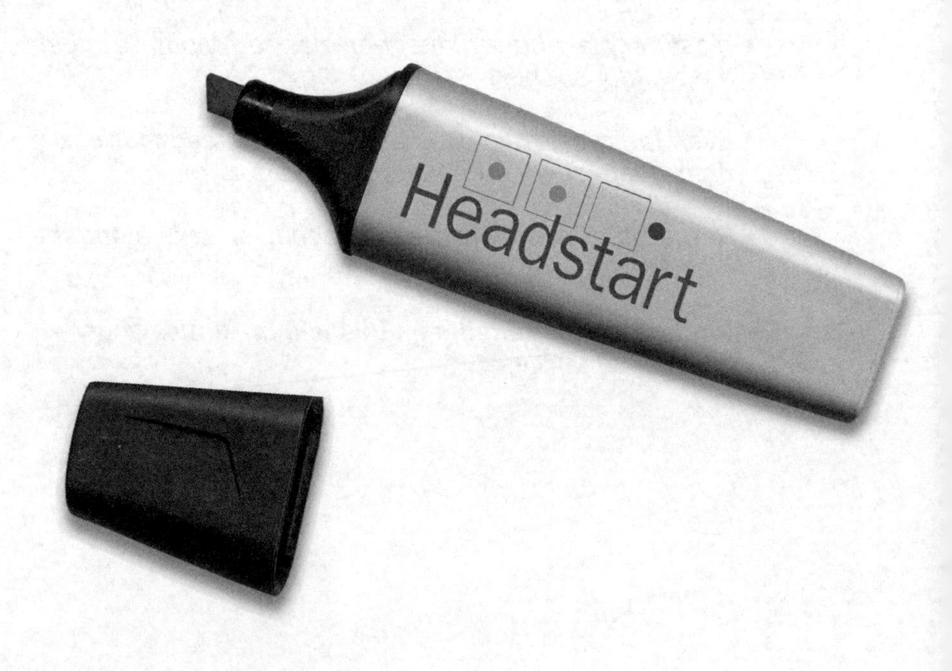
Headstart

CHAPTER 5

BE HUNGRY FOR FEEDBACK

VISION is the BREAKFAST OF CHAMPIONS FEEDBACK is the LUNCH and SELF-CORRECTION the DINNER.

Why you should read this chapter:

- Because **increasing self-awareness** is the first step in self-improvement.
- Because **giving and receiving good quality feedback is pivotal** in High Performance.
- And it will **boost your confidence**.
- Because **high performers are open to learning and growing**.
- Because **you will gain some insights** into coaching and how it can benefit you.
- Because **coaching can be pivotal** to personal success.
- Because **feedback can be destructive** when not thought through.

In his book 'The Seven Habits of Highly Effective People' Stephen R Covey wrote:

VISION is the BREAKFAST OF CHAMPIONS FEEDBACK is the LUNCH and SELF-CORRECTION the DINNER

Good quality, balanced feedback is something that High Performers depend on.

Setting yourself up for feedback

A few years ago I was giving a presentation to over 100 people in London. They were a very mixed group and my topic for the morning was Performance Coaching. I asked them a very simple question:

'How many of you have a coach that you meet with, or at least speak to on the phone, at least once a week or once a fortnight?'

Two per cent of that audience raised their hands.

Kriss Akabusi (Olympic Silver and World Gold medallist) was in that audience. My question really resonated with him. As a world-class athlete he had at least three coaches at any one time.

Coaching and positive feedback makes people taller.

at you eat and you
ices. So here's the thing. This
u unless you categorically agree with [illegible] you never will [illegible] Excellent
u don't agree now and know that you never [illegible] Still here? [illegible] guaranteed to set y
own and go off and do something else... Still here? [illegible] This book wi
set of the few - the High Performance mindset that is guaranteed to [illegible]
ent, achievement and happiness. It's up to you What's in it for you? This book wi
that have been proven to make a difference in individual and team performance. And beca
on't find High Performance natural we have to be disciplined to apply what we learn and take
et something else straight right up front. If you want an easy ride to a better richer life STOP RE
ok NOW and accept that what you have is what you will probably end up with . . . The ideas h
e in theory but clearly if they were all so easy to implement everyone would be doing them, w
d they're not. All HIGH PERFORMING, successful PEOPLE that I have met or read about, WORK
LLY REALLY HARD. This stuff is not quick fix. PMA Mohammed Ali was one of the world's greate
n. He was possibly the definitive world champion boxer. Many remember Ali as cocky, even a
istical. They thought he was a cheeky young man who talked a good game. In a recent docum
coach recently said that the sportsman was the hardest working boxer he had ever met BOTH
F THE RING. He trained harder, practised more and of course had INCREDIBLE self-belief. Ali ha
just PMA, which stands for Positive Mental Attitude, by the way. Do you think PMA is a good th
you do. So do I. But let's be honest here, having a PMA does not guarantee success. For exa
ided to run in the 100m sprint at the Olympics [illegible] with no specific training, it would not b
all the PMA in the world, you would still be unlikely to win [illegible] PMA you would probably
loser. PMA is part of the deal but it is by no means the answer [illegible] problems. It's up to y
e chief executive of your life. That means you choose what you do, who you spen
th, what you eat and you choose the consequences of those choices. It's up to yo
ance People make a habit of doing [illegible] unsuccessful people find uncomfortable. C
ave met thousands of amazing people with [illegible] natural talent. Yet few of them fulfil thei
many never even recognise their gifts. They simply go [illegible] In fact, most people appear to
would call NEAR LIFE EXPERIENCES. They are always about to make the big change, but some
busy. They think [illegible] and to doing it TOMORROW. If anyone ever says 'I'll start my
orrow', or 'I'll give up [illegible] they are not committed. If it's worth doing it's wor
WIN Disease (I Want It Now) You know [illegible] rocket science. The things that make a real di
life are remarkably easy to understand and [illegible] your grasp right now. But the
Most of us are 'bone idle'. Have you noticed how many [illegible] want an easy rout
d financial freedom? They will happily buy a product called Slim [illegible] because they are con
solve their weight problem deep down they know that slimming is a combination of de
upport, discipline, drive and [illegible] takes time to reach a target weight, to adjust a met
ge a lifestyle. And even though they [illegible] EFFORT AND HARD WORK will probabl
iovascular risks and give them more energy for a [illegible] still buy Slim Quick. Come o
t daft, just lazy!!! It's up to you High Performance People make a habit of doing the
successful people find uncomfortable.It's up to you 80/20 [illegible] expect you will have hea
20 theory beforeIn simple terms it says that 80% of profits, results, inventions or whatever com
of the population. This law holds true in every environment I have encountered through my w
re. When I run my seminars, after the students have had three days learning motivational and
s on performance, I ask the following question: Based on Pareto's law I know that only 20% o
do anything different when you leave this seminar. Show me by raising your hand if you will
Guess what? Every hand goes up. Yet I know that the law will hold true. 80% will do nothing
ll do diddlysquat. Every day, thousands of books like this one are bought (though not read n
e listen to CDs and attend seminars all the time, yet very few of them actually do anything dif
Why should this be? As I said earlier, WE CRAVE FOR SOMETHING MORE. But somehow we
ered to go and get it. It's somehow easier to settle for what we have and live a NEAR LIFE exp
this: You will probably live for 80 years based upon current medical developments. If you NE
u really want for the rest of your life how will you feel? If the Pareto Principle is true then you
effort if you want to be in that 20%. A bit of effort is all it takes. And you may spend the res
even more happiness and fulfilment, which you deserve by the way. It's up to you M
It's up to you I was recently on holiday in France and spent some time with the Ma
any. Peter was only 21 but was easily the most professional holiday company repres
developed a problem with the brakes and Peter had willingly gone the e
himself to organise a swift service at a good price. On the wa
first joined his company when he had been just 18 y

Be hungry for feedback

Top class athletes almost always have more than one coach and they will see them virtually every day. They will have a coach to help them with their skill and technique. They will have another to help them work on strategy and a third coach helps them with the psychological aspect of the sport as well as the sportsman's attitude. They are often referred to as mind coaches. Dr Bob Rotella is a mind coach. He has helped dozens of world-class golfers achieve the kind of major success that they were unlikely to have been able to reach without his input.

So, why, in the business world, do we often refuse coaching? Why do we often consider it to be interference or an imposition?

And why is coaching important anyway?

As a manager and trainer in the pharmaceutical industry I was responsible for the training and development of many professional sales people. The minute I suggested that a Sales Representative had a COACH accompany him, it was as if I had asked him to see a psychiatrist.

'Why? What's wrong with me?' the Representative would say. It was as if my suggestion implied that they were somehow flawed or under performing.

Well obviously, sometimes this was the case but more often than not we were simply fine tuning already excellent performance. Coaching makes people perform better. It is a simple as that. A squash player would never act so defensively, when offered a coach. He would be thrilled. Think about it. Where's the difference?

One of our Executive Sales Representatives, Dave Brownlee, was always open to coaching and welcomed feedback and ideas.

Dave, by the way, had consistently been one of the company's top performers for more than 30 years. Fancy that!

The truth is that 'coach' is often the label given to a person whose job it is to criticise and correct. So coaching in the corporate world gets a bad name (but that's a whole other book!). A good coach can be an excellent sounding board and will be able to offer high quality and well-structured feedback that all High Performers thrive on.

But I digress.

Kriss's presence in the audience that day had a major impact on me.

What sticks in my mind is that although Kriss might have previously worked with several sports coaches, until that day he had never had a business coach. After hearing me speak, he soon did. He attributes much of his success of his flourishing speaking business to his openness to learn, be coached and get feedback.

Since that day, I have had the pleasure of working closely with Kriss - who is, today, one of the UK's top motivational speakers. One of his many outstanding qualities is his hunger for feedback and self-improvement.

I remember one meeting we attended together with a big client of his. The meeting went well; we agreed the deal and the event was to go ahead.

One hour later, Kriss rang me to discuss our performance. He wanted to know what I thought we did well and what we could have done better. The call lasted over an hour.

The little boy who listened

In sport, coaching is an accepted part of the game. So, let me help you to understand the value of coaching and feedback in the context of sport.

I started out as a squash coach when I was just 17 years old. I was responsible for coaching the juniors at Gateshead Squash Club.

Every Saturday morning, 15 or 20 children aged from five to 15 would be dropped off at the club to be left in my young but capable hands.

Looking back, I can see that this should have been a daunting challenge for someone of my age, but at the time it just seemed the right thing to do. I loved it. I was passionate about my sport and equally passionate about creating great players.

One particular Saturday a guy I knew quite well brought his six year old son David along for the nine o' clock session. Our conversation went something like this (I have translated it from the original Geordie for your benefit, of course).

'Can you coach my lad?' asked the dad, standing beside his silent, shy son, who had not even been brave enough to look at me yet.

'Of course. How old is he?' I replied.

'He's only six.'

'That shouldn't be a problem. We have a five year old on court now so he'll enjoy it.'

'I must warn you, Steve, He's hopeless at ball sports. He has no coordination. I hope he doesn't hold the others back.'

The dad just looked at me as though David wasn't even there. David, of course, said nothing. No reaction. He just stood still with his head down and stayed quiet.

Even at the age of only 17, I felt sure that this was not the right way to speak about your child in front of him. I can remember wondering whether the father had even considered that his son could hear him. I did not think it was my place to say anything, after all this was his dad speaking.

'Does David have a racket?' I asked quickly trying to move the conversation onto something more positive.

'No, he's never been any good at this hand-eye stuff so we couldn't see the point.'

'Well, we'll give him a chance, shall we? See if he enjoys it?' And young David joined the group.

His dad was right. David was hopeless and could barely lift the racket. I would kneel down beside him in an attempt to get eye contact. I would ask him to raise his racket to be ready to swing it. Sure enough his racket would go up in the air, but then, by the time I had stood up, it had slowly dipped back to the floor. I can only describe it like watching a slowly deflating balloon.

This kid had a long way to go and squash was the last thing on the agenda. But I was not going to give up on him.

I gave consistent and abundant positive feedback. Every time David made an effort, got close, or even spoke he got praise.

Six weeks later, which was, in fact, just six one-hour sessions later, David was hitting the ball gently, but consistently. He was joining in with the other kids.

Over the years I have met a lot of people of all ages on the squash court. I have never yet met anyone who cannot hit a squash ball with a squash racket.

Be hungry for feedback

The first time David hit the ball I watched him change. It was as if he grew in front of my eyes. I saw him double in height when he hit that ball. His demeanour changed completely. I now know that coaching and positive feedback have the power to make people feel taller.

Coaching and positive feedback makes people taller

Of course there is another message in this story: be careful what you teach your children. They are like sponges and they hear and listen to everything you say. They listen especially to conversations that you have about them, but not with them.

This kind of Passive Feedback is not useful. In fact it's down right destructive. It will destroy self-esteem and create, at best, average results.

Well thought through and constructive feedback is essential for growth - just like food and water. When they are done well it makes a huge difference.

Benefits of balanced feedback

Regular doses of well constructed feedback will:

- Increase self-awareness
- Highlight strengths
- Build self-esteem
- Build confidence
- Improve performance

Being hungry for feedback is a High Performance trait, but High Performers don't just seek out the rose-tinted stuff, the positive feedback, they need to know it all, so that they can develop proactive strategies for success.

Note to reader:
This book is not intended to show you how to coach. However, if you are to understand the value of feedback it is useful to look at how great feedback should be given. Take it as read that ALL HIGH PERFORMERS seek out and expect feedback to achieve success.

How to give feedback

Telling someone they are right or wrong, good or bad is not helpful. It can result in closing people down and making them very defensive.

Think of the last time you did something really daft. Maybe you backed your car into a bollard? There is nothing more infuriating than some 'friend' telling you how 'that was a stupid thing to do' and that 'the next time you need to be more careful.'

You already know it was stupid. And being more careful is probably a strategy you could work out for yourself...yeah?

When I first met Louise and she told me the kick-boxing story I shared with you in Chapter Three, I responded with the words:

'So did that work for you?'

This is non judgemental and opens up dialogue brilliantly. Maybe you should try it sometime?

This is just the same principle as the MOB exercise (see Chapter Three). Asking people what is working for them allows them to focus on their strengths and the positive things in their lives.

Getting people to reflect on their success strategies is crucial to performance enhancement.

So ask yourself:

What is working for you right now?
AND
Now ask, what is not working?

Be hungry for feedback

Let's try it right now:

Note down here five things that are working for you right now. Think about both personal and business. Be Honest.

Now note down five things that you are doing and are NOT working. Where are you getting frustrated, losing interest or becoming disengaged?

Now consider the difference between the two.

* What is happening when things work well?
* Who are you with if anyone?
* What is the task or activity?
* Are you having fun?
* Are you in the Flow?

You see how this is far less personal and much more constructive. Even a quick self assessment based on these simple questions can raise your self awareness and set you up for an inspiring goal.

The key is to be honest with your self and to only receive feedback from people who are neutral and have a vested interest in your life working.

Be careful of people who ask you if you would you like some feedback. Do you trust the person who offers it? On occasion it may be a cunning plan to criticise your performance.

Generally, people are not good at telling you what they really think. Maybe they don't want to hurt your feelings, and instead tell you what they think you want to hear? Maybe they have their own agenda, and won't say you are ideal for a certain job because they want to apply for it themselves?

Maybe they just can't be bothered to listen carefully and prepare useful comments for you, and resort to saying 'that's fine' just to shut you up and move onto another topic.

Most people would rather be nice than helpful – and so they keep the real, warts and all, truth to themselves.

How to give feedback

Let's face it those honest, harsh facts are often the most helpful and kinder in the long run, aren't they?

If you are a parent, you will know that you can only afford to give your children good, honest feedback. You have to do that because you want them to be safe and free from harm. As we grow up and become adults, we get soft and less able to take truly honest feedback. But if you hold back the truth with an adult you are still harming them.

You can learn to treat giving honest feedback as a great opportunity to build the self-esteem of the recipient.

I remember a time when Anna was about two years old. She was at the age where she was continually testing things out to find out what she could get away with and what she couldn't. She was just like any normal toddler. She would try out her drawing skills on the walls. Something Christopher our oldest, never did.

Most people would rather be nice than helpful – and so they keep the real, warts and all, truth to themselves.

'That's a very naughty thing to do for such a beautiful little princess,' I would say.

This was my way of detaching the feedback from Anna and attaching it, instead, to her action. By giving feedback like that, I could say that what she did was a naughty thing but that she was still OK.

So be careful, too, to detach the negative action from the person. For example, you would not say: 'You are a hopeless presenter.' Instead, you would say: 'Your presentation was maybe not as ... fast/slow/slick/whatever ... as it could be.' Then you could go on to suggest ways to make the presentation better next time.

'That is a beautiful wall - but it is maybe not as straight as it could be. How might you approach X, Y or Z differently if you were doing it again?'

As a rule, when you give feedback, you should try to think of something good to say first, and then go on to attend to areas for improvement.

The person to whom you are giving feedback might be suffering from low self-esteem. If that's true, and you tell them they are a 'bad presenter', just as I might have told Anna she was a 'naughty girl', it could have a negative long-term impact.

Telling the amateur stonemason that he is a 'bad builder' could mean that he never attempts to build a wall again.

In many respects my wife, Abby, is my best coach. After all, someone has to motivate the motivator. We can all benefit from having someone to help us get up and out in the morning.

Objective feedback

As I mentioned earlier, the people you choose to give you feedback should have a vested interest in your life working. A coach need not necessarily know you that well but he will have a general belief in human potential and will not limit your dreams or aspirations. You can benefit from having a coach who comes from outside your environment. In this way he or she can be totally objective and useful for 'out of the box' creative thinking.

Tell it like it is

In his book '*Primal Leadership*', Daniel Goleman writes about Emotional Intelligence. He tells us that in a study of qualitative feedback in organisations, they found some interesting facts.

Apparently, Senior Managers, who feed down the line to their subordinates, would generally give positive, if not 'rose-tinted' feedback about what was going on in their department.

Meanwhile the workforce, the subordinates, themselves did not see things in quite the same way. In reality, the workforce would probably have a number of problems and issues but would not tell their managers about them.

This is one big reason why Chief Executives and Directors of organisations bring in coaches from outside the organisation. They do it because they can guarantee real, honest feedback.

As an individual you should be aware of this but you should not have the same problem as you are choosing your support team and therefore those who will be feeding back.

In another of Goleman's studies they contrasted non-evaluative feedback with more honest open and full feedback.

MBA Students were put into groups and would give feedback to each other at the end of each week. Each person would then comment on the three most useful bits of feedback he or she had received.

Contrary to the thinking at the time, which was that if you soften feedback it will be better received, the consensus was that the evaluative feedback given candidly about specific areas that worked and didn't work were far more helpful.

You asked for it!

Over the years I have learned that top performers are always hungry for feedback. Not just open to it but hungry for it. They also want the truth, not a watered down version.

Be hungry for feedback

High Performers seek out opportunities for honest feedback. They do this regularly and because it is structured around what's working and what's not working rather than what's good or bad it maintains their self-esteem and confidence. It also massively increases their self-awareness.

High Performance People recognise that they will have off days and will not always perform at their peak. They want feedback so that they can continually improve.

Who would you like to be on the credits of your life movie?

SIXTY SECOND SUMMARY

- *Well constructed feedback is essential for growth and improvement.*
- *High performers seek out feedback and act on it!*
- *Two powerful questions to ask: What's working? What's not working?*
- *Kids hear everything you say - good or bad.*
- *Positive feedback builds self-esteem.*
- *Most people would rather be nice than helpful.*

Headstart

CHAPTER 6

CREATE YOUR DREAM TEAM

To be the best you need to mix with the best.

ose what yo[illegible]
at you eat and you ch[illegible]
oices. So here's the thing. This bo[illegible]
you unless you categorically agree with bo[illegible]
you don't agree now and know that you never will, the[illegible]
down and go off and do something else... Still here? Excellent!
dset of the few - the High Performance mindset that is guaranteed to set you
nent, achievement and happiness. **It's up to you** What's in it for you? This book will c
as that have been proven to make a difference in individual and team performance. And beca
don't find High Performance natural we have to be disciplined to apply what we learn and tak
get something else straight right up front. If you want an easy ride to a better richer life STOP R
ook NOW and accept that what you have is what you will probably end up with . . . The ideas
le in theory but clearly if they were all so easy to implement everyone would be doing them,
nd they're not. All HIGH PERFORMING, successful PEOPLE that I have met or read about, WOR
ALLY REALLY HARD. This stuff is not quick fix. PMA Mohammed Ali was one of the world's grea
en. He was possibly the definitive world champion boxer. Many remember Ali as cocky, even
otistical. They thought he was a cheeky young man who talked a good game. In a recent docu
coach recently said that the sportsman was the hardest working boxer he had ever met BOT
OF THE RING. He trained harder, practised more and of course had INCREDIBLE self-belief. Ali h
just PMA, which stands for Positive Mental Attitude, by the way. Do you think PMA is a good
e you do. So do I. But let's be honest, here. Having a PMA does not guarantee success. For ex
cided to run in the 100m sprint at the Olympics right now, with no specific training, it would no
d all the PMA in the world, you would still be unlikely to win. But with PMA you would probab
y loser. PMA is part of the deal but it is by no means the answer to your problems. **It's up to**
he chief executive of your life. That means you choose what you do, who you spe
with, what you eat and [illegible] the consequences of those choices. It's up to
mance People make a habit of doing the things that unsuccessful people find uncomfortable.
have met thousands of amazing people with [illegible] natural talent. Yet few of them fulfil th
many never even recognise their gifts. They simply go [illegible] In fact most people appear t
I would call NEAR LIFE EXPERIENCES. They are always about to make a change, but som
oo busy. They think [illegible] round to doing it TOMORROW. If anyone [illegible] says 'I'll start m
morrow', or 'I'll give up smoking next week,' they are not committed. If it's worth doing it's wo
IWIN Disease (I Want It Now) You know this is not rocket science. The things that make a real d
ur life are remarkably easy to understand and they lie well within your grasp right now. But th
ch: Most of us are 'bone idle' Have you noticed how many people [illegible] want an easy rou
and financial freedom? They will happily buy a product called Slim Quick because they are co
esolve their weight problems, [illegible] keep down they know that slimming is a combination of d
support, discipline, drive and motivation. It takes time to reach a target weight, to adjust a me
nge a lifestyle. And even though they know that it requires EFFORT AND HARD WORK will probab
diovascular risks and give them more energy [illegible] they still buy Slim Quick. Come
n't daft, just lazy!!! **It's up to you High Performance People make a habit of doing th**
nsuccessful people find uncomfortable. It's up to you 80/20 I expect you will have he
0/20 theory beforeIn simple terms it says that 80% of profits, results, inventions or whatever co
% of the population. This law holds true in every environment I have encountered through my
sure. When I run my seminars, after the students have had three days learning motivational an
as on performance, I ask the following question: Based on Pareto's law I know that only 20%
y do anything different when you leave this seminar. Show me by raising your hand if you wil
%. Guess what? Every hand goes up. Yet I know that the law will hold true. 80% will do nothing
will do diddlysquat. Every day, thousands of books like this one are bought (though not read
ple listen to CDs and attend seminars all the time, yet very few of them actually do anything d
lt. Why should this be? As I said earlier, WE CRAVE FOR SOMETHING MORE. But somehow w
hered to go and get it. It's somehow easier to settle for what we have and live a NEAR LIFE e
er this: You will probably live for 80 years based upon current medical developments. If you t
ou really want for the rest of your life how will you feel? If the Pareto Principle is true then yo
e an effort if you want to be in that 20%. A bit of effort is all it takes. And you may spend the r
s enjoying even more happiness and fulfilment, which you deserve by the way. It's up to you
e idle' **It's up to you** I was recently on holiday in France and spent some time with the M
Peter was only 21 but was easily the most professional holiday company repr
developed a problem with the brakes and Peter had willingly gone the
himself to organise a swift service at a good price. On the w
first joined his company when he had been just 18
posh suit so he would look his best (he
prepared a file of his achieve
the questions and
he wait

Why you should read this chapter:

- Because **no-one ever achieved anything great on their own**.
- Because the **people** you choose to surround yourself with can and **will influence your life**, for better or for worse.
- Because you **need to have the support of like-minded people** who have a vested interest in your life working.

Having a coach is definitely going to increase your chances of achieving your goals but whether you have a coach or not you definitely need a support network of some kind to help your on your journey to success.

As I mentioned earlier, you have to do it by yourself but you cannot do it alone.

If you have ever watched the Oscars you get the idea. Every winner of an Academy Award has at least two dozen people to thank for their personal achievement.

Many times, having just watched a fantastic movie, I am amazed at the length of the credits. Hundreds of assistants, makeup artists and other experts have worked behind the scenes to make a one and a half hour film. How many people do you need to help you to achieve what you want for a lifetime?

Who would you like to be on the credits of your life movie?

Mix with the best

I started my working life in 1981 and soon learned a great lesson about high performance and achievement. I learned that:

To be the best you need to mix with the best

Many years ago, I took a job selling life assurance with Legal & General. The first video they showed me clearly stated that if you want to enjoy success you need to mix with like-minded, optimistic, successful people. This principle has stayed with me ever since, and served me well in all areas of my life.

Create your Dream Team

Remember my squash experience? When I took up squash at 15 years old, I set myself the goal of becoming the Northumberland County Champion. I soon met the then Under-19 champion and set about practising and training with him. Each time we played, he thrashed me. He won easily. It was very painful for my ego but I knew that I was learning how the current champion performed.

One evening when I was practising, I noticed a crowd of spectators watching a player on another court. I could see that there were far too many people watching for this to be an ordinary match. The young guy on court turned out to be Bryan Beeson, who was then our club's Number One player. In fact, five or six years later he became the British Champion.

I think you can guess what happened next: I made a beeline for Bryan. I began playing him more than anyone else. I spent as many hours as I could chatting to him watching him, learning from him. Bryan soon became one of my closest friends and mentors.

Within a few months of setting my goal to become County Champion, I had developed a circle of squash playing friends who were all dedicated, focused, competitive and encouraging.

A year after I first picked up a racket, and after much practising and training - and, of course, losing - I became the Northumberland County Under-19 Champion.

Do you think I achieved this goal because I had a natural talent for squash? I don't. I reached that level because I was very clear about what I wanted. I was so passionate about squash. I trained every day, I worked really hard, I mixed with like-minded, top performers, and was determined to succeed.

Who matters?

Think of a goal you have, a dream, an ambition. Write it down.

____

____

____

____

Create your Dream Team

Consider whom you know already in this field. Who are the experts? Who has experience? Write down their names.

____

____

____

____

____

Consider whom you spend most of your time with right now. Write down their names.

____

____

____

____

____

Does the first set of names match the second set of names? It ought to.

If the sets of names do not match, then consider why this might be. Start investing your time in developing a network of people in the field in which you want to excel.

What happens when you mix with the worst

If you choose to mix with people who are world-class complainers, moaners and whiners, you will almost certainly find yourself being dragged down to their level of thinking and behaving. Or at best you will feel drained and deflated.

I have some female friends who are single and looking for love. Their goal is to find the man of their dreams and settle down just the like the 'Lady from Oprah'.

‘Nothing of any significance was ever created by being realistic.’

- Tony Robbins

These same people often spend all weekend talking and socialising with girl friends in a similar situation. They will often reflect on the great night they had talking about how difficult it is to find a good man. They find solace by socialising with other singles who are bitter about their negative experiences and spend their time complaining about the opposite sex and recounting their disasters. This will serve one purpose - it justifies their views but it does not move them closer to their dream.

Just as we have seen in the earlier scenario, mixing with negative people will only infect you, and affirm your beliefs that good relationships are impossible to find.

If you want to meet the ideal partner you should avoid singles clubs, but instead mix with happily married couples, learn about them, listen to them, watch them together. Find out that good relationships exist and go out and find yourself a date.

People who seem to take pleasure in hearing about your failures are psychic vampires or as Michael Breen calls them Mood Hoovers. They suck the ambition out of you. They will tell you to wise up and face the nasty truth. They will tell you to be realistic. You don't want these people in your team.

'Nothing of any significance was ever created by being realistic.'
– Tony Robbins

If you want something, mix with the people who are already doing what you want to do and are doing it well.

At one point Kriss Akabusi decided to change his specialist event from 400 metre hurdles to 400 metre flat. The people around him told him it could not be done. Kriss didn't listen. Instead, he found the best people in his new chosen field, trained with Edwin Moses, the world's greatest ever 400 metre hurdler. Akabusi won a Silver medal at the 1984 Olympics and 2 bronze medals 8 years later.

Who do you spend time with?

Think of whom you spend time with. Write down their names here. They may be the same people you noted down earlier in this chapter.

____

____

____

____

Now, from the start of next week make a note of the first 10 people you meet. They can be new or existing contacts. Beside their name, make a note about how you feel when you are with them. Are they nurturing, supportive, toxic or draining? Do they listen to you? Or do they talk about themselves? Do you feel energised and raring to go after spending time with them or worn out?

____

____

____

____

Do not encourage negative people into your life. Minimise or eliminate these people from your life. You cannot afford to spend time with people who have a vested interest in your life failing.

Who do you want in your Dream Team?

High Performance People create themselves a Dream Team or Support Team They surround themselves with coaches, supporters, motivators and mentors who can help them to succeed.

Each member of your own Dream Team must have a vested interest in you and in each other. Belonging to such a team virtually guarantees you above-average performance.

Very successful entrepreneurs, like Richard Branson and Bill Gates, surround themselves with people who have talents they do not possess themselves. Great leaders accept from the start that they don't know everything. By having this support network and admitting that they cannot do it all alone, they take the pressure off themselves.

The first person you will have in your Dream Team of course is you. You now have to heavily invest your time in establishing relationships with other crucial people.

Even before I started my business I became involved in a support team. We held our first meeting in December 4th 2001 when I was still in my full-time job as Head of Sales Training.

Later that month, after nearly 16 years of very secure employment, 18 months later than I had expected, I left my job. I felt vulnerable. The camaraderie and teamwork that I had experienced in corporate life would not be coming with me into the isolated world of self-employment, and I recognised that I would have to recreate it somehow.

I wanted to find a way to create a familiar environment, so I became part of a group of like-minded people - a group of people who would all support each other, even though their businesses might be very different. We created relationships, which to this day have been invaluable to me and my success. We discuss our businesses, our aspirations, needs and problems. Everything we talk about is completely safe and confidential.

Today the team has evolved. Much of my communication is by phone and through one to ones, when we manage to meet up face to face with another team member.

In my team I have Kriss Akabusi, who motivates me and asks great questions. Then I have Nigel Risner who gives excellent feedback and adds huge value with his creative business ideas. I also have Lesley Everett who shares business objectives and was instrumental in this book getting off the ground. And Paul McGee who has an almost identical situation to mine as far as aspirations, family situation and so on are concerned. We talk to each other regularly about our plans and reassure each other that we are on track. Marie Mosely is a true friend without whom I would never have started my speaking career. Marie is my constant advocate and supporter. Paul Bridle is an expert in leadership and a first class coach. He is awesome at asking the right question at just the right time and offering feedback exactly as I described it earlier.

Get the idea?

Building your Dream Team takes T.I.M.E.©

Create your Dream Team

Selecting the right people for your Dream Team can be a challenge. As I said, it is vital that your Team is made up of people who will be as passionate as you are about the success of your business. To this end, I have come up with my own formula to help you pick the right people.

Once again, children have been my inspiration. Have you ever realised that children spell love T.I.M.E.?

Deep down, they don't want presents or trips to the cinema to show that you love them - particularly if it is not you who takes them. What they want, quite simply, is your TIME. The more time you spend with them, the more time you invest in your relationship, the more they will KNOW you love them.

I believe that time is vital for all relationships, whether they are personal or professional. You must learn to invest your time in the people who matter most.

Building your Dream Team takes T.I.M.E. ©

My formula to help me pick my Dream Team members is also spelled T.I.M.E. It's an easy acronym to remember and will enable you to develop trust and team spirit among your members. Here it is:

T Trust
I Integrity
M Mutual benefit
E Empathy

Trust

Trust is the core ingredient in any successful relationship. If two people do not trust each other, their relationship is on shaky ground from the start. Mutual trust is imperative. Many communication workshops that I have attended, and now lead, focus on the importance of trust.

Integrity

Integrity is equally important. Each Dream Team member must live according to his or her own values, just as you do. Everyone must be what I call authentic. This means real and true to themselves.

Create your Dream Team

Without trust and integrity you do not have a Team member, so before we go any further, here is an exercise that I do on my Step in the Right Direction Programme and that I would like to share with you now. Use it to help you to choose the right people:

You will find that the next page is headed with the words Brilliant Relationship. Think of a relationship you have or have had which is brilliant. On this page write down all the things that made that relationship so good. What happened that made it work?

On the second page, headed Terrible Relationship you need to think of the worst relationship you have experienced and write down all the things that happened to make it so bad.

Before you go any further, complete these two pages.

BRILLIANT RELATIONSHIP

TERRIBLE RELATIONSHIP

Now let's have a look at what you wrote down. I have done this exercise with hundreds of people and every time the words Trust and Integrity appear on the Brilliant Relationship chart and words like Lack of Trust and Lack of Integrity end up on the Terrible Relationship chart. Funny that. Now are you convinced?
The truth is without Trust and Integrity there will be no relationship. Now let's continue with our TIME acronym.

Mutual benefit

Mutual benefit means that everyone joins the Dream Team with the belief that everyone is equal, and that everyone will benefit from the relationship you develop. You need to believe in win-win. Not only should the Team believe in win-win for everyone, but every member should live his or her life, and work on this principle, too.

The mindset of mutual benefit is founded on the belief that there is always enough business to go around. Dream Team members believe in a basic life law. Let me explain in more detail:

I remember I was coaching one of my corporate clients about their main annual conference. Right at the start the conference team briefed me and told me they needed a speaker for the main event. Now I am a speaker, and this was my client so I could easily have pushed my way in. But instead I recommended Nigel Risner who they subsequently booked. Nigel has since given me equally good opportunities that I otherwise would never have had.

The more you give the more you get

One element of this mutual benefit mindset can be seen clearly when you consider networking. We all have to network in order to grow our businesses - but many people have a problem with the idea of going out among a group of strangers, touting for business.

When you have a mutual benefit mindset, you don't see networking that way. Go into networking situations focusing not on what you want to get, but instead on what you want to give. Listen to people, hear what they have to say and see what you might be able to give them by helping them find what they need.

Connect the people you meet with someone you know, for example. Some of the most powerful gifts you can give cost you nothing at all. The more you give in this way, the more you will gain in the long run. And giving will help to boost your self-esteem at the same time.

Some of the most powerful gifts you can give cost you nothing at all

And finally . . .

Empathy

Empathy for each other is vital. Each member must be in touch with his or her own emotions, as well as those of the rest of the Dream Team. You must be able to see the world from someone else's point of view.

To belong to the Dream Team, you need to be willing and able to put yourself in another's shoes. This is not just about mutual benefit; it is also about truly wanting to understand.

If you know someone who fits the T.I.M.E. model, and find that you both benefit from the huge amount of mutual trust you create from living with integrity; if you find that you both work for each other's benefit and genuinely want to understand each other and your businesses, and that you find yourself being of real help to him; then you should seriously consider making that person part of your Dream Team.

Pick your Dream Team now

Write a list of the people you know now who are strong contenders for your support team. Think about how often you see them or make contact at the moment. Think what you could offer to them that would enhance their lives or businesses.

____

____

____

____

____

____

____

____

Some of the most powerful gifts you can give cost you nothing at all.

ose what yo[illegible]
at you eat and you c[illegible]
oices. So here's the thing. This b[illegible]
ou unless you categorically agree with bo[illegible]
ou don't agree now and know that you never will, th[illegible]
down and go off and do something else... Still here? Excellent[illegible]
dset of the few - the High Performance mindset that is guaranteed to set yo[illegible]
nent, achievement and happiness. It's up to you What's in it for you? This book will [illegible]
s that have been proven to make a difference in individual and team performance. And beca
don't find High Performance natural we have to be disciplined to apply what we learn and tak
get something else straight right up front. If you want an easy ride to a better richer life STOP R
ook NOW and accept that what you have is what you will probably end up with . . . The ideas
e in theory but clearly if they were all so easy to implement everyone would be doing them,
nd they're not. All HIGH PERFORMING, successful PEOPLE that I have met or read about, WOR
ALLY REALLY HARD. This stuff is not quick fix. PMA Mohammed Ali was one of the world's grea
en. He was possibly the definitive world champion boxer. Many remember Ali as cocky, even
otistical. They thought he was a cheeky young man who talked a good game. In a recent docu
coach recently said that the sportsman was the hardest working boxer he had ever met BOT
F THE RING. He trained harder, practised more and of course had INCREDIBLE self-belief. Ali h
just PMA, which stands for Positive Mental Attitude, by the way. Do you think PMA is a good
e you do. So c[illegible] But let's be honest, here. Having a PMA does not guarantee success. For ex
cided to run in [illegible] at the Olympics right now, with no specific training, it would no
all the PMA in the w[illegible] [illegible]ld still be unlikely to win. But with PMA you would probabl
y loser. PMA is part of the deal b[illegible] it is [illegible] the answer to your problems. It's up to
e chief executive of your life. That means you choose what you do, who you spe
vith, what you eat and you choose the conseque[illegible] [illegible] choices. It's up to
mance People [illegible] a habit of doing the things that unsuccessful [illegible] comfortable.
ave met thou[illegible] people with AWESOME natural talent. Yet [illegible] them fulfil the
many never even recog[illegible] simply go unused. In fact, most people appear t
I would call NEAR LIFE EXPERIENCES. They are alw[illegible] to make the big change, but som
o busy. They think they will get round to doing it T[illegible]W. If anyone ever says 'I'll start m
orrow', or 'I'll give up smoking next week,' they [illegible] not [illegible]ed. [illegible] worth doing it's wo
WIN Disease (I [illegible] Now) You know, this is not rocket science. The [illegible] make a real c
r life are remar[illegible] [illegible]ersta]nd and they lie well within your grasp r[illegible] now. But the
h: Most of us are 'bone idle'. Have you noticed how many people seem to want an easy rou
nd financial freedom? They will happily buy [illegible] product called Slim Quick because they are co
esolve their weight problems, yet deep down they [illegible] slimming is a combination of d
support, discipline, drive and motivation. It takes time to re[illegible] target weight, to adjust a me
ge a lifestyle. And even though they know that all this EFFORT AND [illegible] WORK will probab
diovascular risks and give them more energy for a longer life, they still buy Slim Quick. Come
't daft, just lazy!!! It's up to you High Performance People make a habit of doing th
nsuccessful people find uncomfortable. It's up to you 80/20 I expect you will have he
0/20 theory beforeIn simple terms it says that 80% of traffic, results, inventions or whatever c
o of the population. This law holds true in every environment I have ever encountered through my
ure. When I run my seminars, after the students have had three days learning motivational an
as on performance, I ask the following question: Based on Pareto's law I know that only 20%
do anything different when you leave this seminar. Show me by raising your hand if you will
Guess what? Every hand goes up. Yet I know that the law will hold true. 80% will do nothing
vill do diddlysquat. Every day, thousands of books like this one are bought (though not read
ple listen to CDs and attend seminars all the time, yet very few of them actually do anything d
t. Why should this be? As I said earlier, WE CRAVE FOR SOMETHING MORE. But somehow we
ered to go and get it. It's somehow easier to settle for what we have and live a NEAR LIFE ex
r this: You will probably live for 80 years based upon current medical developments. If you N
ou really want for the rest of your life how will you feel? If the Pareto Principle is true then you
e an effort if you want to be in that 20%. A bit of effort is all it takes. And you may spend the r
enj[illegible]g even more happiness and fulfilment, which you deserve by the way. It's up to you
e idle' It's up to you I was recently on holiday in France and spent some time with the M
ny. Peter was only 21 but was easily the most professional holiday company repre
developed a problem with the brakes and Peter had willingly gone the
himself to organise a swift service at a good price. On the w
first joined his company when he had been just 18
posh suit so he would look his best (he
prepared a file of his achieve
the questions and
he waite

Create your Dream Team

Write down the names of three people you believe to have the T.I.M.E. to be in your Dream Team.

Write down the names of three people you do not consider to have the T.I.M.E. to be in your Dream Team.

When you start to focus on the right people and the wrong people, you will be well on the way to creating your own team.

ose what y... at you eat and you ... So here's the thing. This ... agree with ... never will ... Excellent ...
oices. So here's the thing. This ... categorically agree with ... you never will ... Excellent ... to set y...
ou unless you categorically agree now and know that you never will ... Still here? Excellent ... guaranteed to set y... This book will
ou don't agree now and know that you never will, ... Still here? ... is guaranteed to set you? This book wi... And beca
down and go off and do something else... Still here? Excellent mindset that is guaranteed to ... performance. And beca
dset of the few - the High Performance mindset that is guaranteed ... What's in it for you? ... what we learn and tak
nent, achievement and happiness. It's up to you What's in it for you? individual and team performance ... richer life STOP R
s that have been proven to make a difference in individual ... disciplined to apply what we learn ... The ideas
don't find High Performance natural we have to be disciplined to ... a better richer life ... doing them,
get something else straight right up front. If you want an easy ride ... probably end up with ... would be doing them, WOR
ook NOW and accept that what you have is what you will probably ... everyone would be ... read about, WOR
e in theory but clearly if they were all so easy to implement everyone ... met or read about, WOR
nd they're not. All HIGH PERFORMING, successful PEOPLE that I have met or read about ... one of the world's grea
ALLY REALLY HARD. This stuff is not quick fix. PMA Mohammed Ali was one of the world's grea
en. He was possibly the definitive world champion boxer. Many remember Ali as cocky, even
otistical. They thought he was a cheeky young man who talked a good game. In a recent docu
coach recently said that the sportsman was the hardest working boxer he had ever met BOTH
OF THE RING. He trained harder, practised more and of course had INCREDIBLE self-belief. Ali h
just PMA, which stands for Positive Mental Attitude, by the way. Do you think PMA is a good t
e you do. So do I. But let's be honest, here. Having a PMA does not guarantee success. For ex
cided to run in the 100m sprint at the Olympics right now, with no specific training, it would not
d all the PMA in the world, you would still be unlikely to win. But with PMA you would probabl
y loser. PMA is part of the deal but it is by no means the answer to your problems. It's up to
e chief executive of your life. That means you choose what you do, who you spe
vith, what you eat and ... the consequences of those choices. It's up to y
nance People make a habit of doing things that unsuccessful people find uncomfortable.
ave met thousands of amazing people with AMAZING natural talent. Yet few of them fulfil the
many never even recognise their gifts. They simply ... In fact most people appear t
I would call NEAR LIFE EXPERIENCES. They are always about to make a change, but som
o busy. They think they will get round to doing it TOMORROW. If anyone ever says 'I'll start m
norrow', or 'I'll give up smoking next week' they are not committed. If it's worth doing it's wo
WIN Disease (I Want It Now) You know it's not rocket science. The things that make a real c
ur life are remarkably easy to understand and they lie well within your grasp right now. But the
h: Most of us are 'bone idle' Have you noticed how many people who want an easy rou
nd financial freedom? They will happily buy a product called Slim Quick because they are co
esolve their weight problems, yet deep down they know that slimming is a combination of de
support, discipline, drive and motivation. It takes time to reach a target weight, to adjust a me
nge a lifestyle. And even though they know that all this EFFORT AND HARD WORK will probab
diovascular risks and give them more energy for a longer life, they still buy Slim Quick. Come
n't daft, just lazy!!! It's up to you High Performance People make a habit of doing th
nsuccessful people find uncomfortable.It's up to you 80/20 I expect you will have he
0/20 theory beforeIn simple terms it says that 80% of profits, results, inventions or whatever co
% of the population. This law holds true in every environment I have encountered through my
ure. When I run my seminars, after the students have had three days learning motivational and
as on performance, I ask the following question: Based on Pareto's law I know that only 20% c
do anything different when you leave this seminar. Show me by raising your hand if you will
. Guess what? Every hand goes up. Yet I know that the law will hold true. 80% will do nothing
ill do diddlysquat. Every day, thousands of books like this one are bought (though not read
ple listen to CDs and attend seminars all the time, yet very few of them actually do anything d
t. Why should this be? As I said earlier, WE CRAVE FOR SOMETHING MORE. But somehow we
ered to go and get it. It's somehow easier to settle for what we have and live a NEAR LIFE ex
r this: You will probably live for 80 years based upon current medical developments. If you N
ou really want for the rest of your life how will you feel? If the Pareto Principle is true then you
e an effort if you want to be in that 20%. A bit of effort is all it takes. And you may spend the re
enjoy even more happiness and fulfilment, which you deserve by the way. It's up to you I
e idle' It's up to you I was recently on holiday in France and spent some time with the M
any. Peter was only 21 but was easily the most professional holiday company repre
... developed a problem with the brakes and Peter had willingly gone the
... himself to organise a swift service at a good price. On the w
... first joined his company when he had been just 18
... posh suit so he would look his best (he
... prepared a file of his achieve
... the questions and a
... he waite

The more you give the more you get.

SIXTY SECOND SUMMARY

- *Even Steve Redgrave never achieved an Olympic Gold Medal alone.*
- *High performers get loads of support.*
- *Positive support can keep you going when your motivation is low.*
- *Beware of psychic vampires.*
- *Children spell love TIME.*
- *TIME is a formula for Dream team candidates.*

  Trust
  Integrity
  Mutual Benefit
  Empathy

- *Be prepared to give and you will receive. This is the law of abundance.*

Headstart

CHAPTER 7

MODEL WHAT YOU WANT

You get what you model.

ose what ...
hat you eat and you ... the thing. This ...
oices. So here's the thing. This ... agree with ...
ou unless you categorically agree with ... never will, ...
you don't agree now and know that you never will, ... Excellent ... to set y...
down and go off and do something else... Still here? Excellent...
dset of the few - the High Performance mindset that is guaranteed to set y...
nent, achievement and happiness. It's up to you What's in it for you? This book wi...
as that have been proven to make a difference in individual and team performance. And beca...
don't find High Performance natural we have to be disciplined to apply what we learn and tal...
get something else straight right up front. If you want an easy ride to a better richer life STOP I...
ook NOW and accept that what you have is what you will probably end up with . . . The ideas...
le in theory but clearly if they were all so easy to implement everyone would be doing them, ...
nd they're not. All HIGH PERFORMING, successful PEOPLE that I have met or read about, WOR...
ALLY REALLY HARD. This stuff is not quick fix. PMA Mohammed Ali was one of the world's grea...
en. He was possibly the definitive world champion boxer. Many remember Ali as cocky, even...
otistical. They thought he was a cheeky young man who talked a good game. In a recent docu...
coach recently said that the sportsman was the hardest working boxer he had ever met BOT...
OF THE RING. He trained harder, practised more and of course had INCREDIBLE self-belief. Ali h...
n just PMA, which stands for Positive Mental Attitude, by the way. Do you think PMA is a good...
e you do. So do I. But let's be honest, here. Having a PMA does not guarantee success. For e...
cided to run in the 100m sprint at the Olympics right now, with no specific training, it would no...
d all the PMA in the world, you would still be unlikely to win. But with PMA you would probab...
y loser. PMA is part of the deal but it is by no means the answer to your problems. It's up to...
he chief executive of your life. That means you choose what you do, who you spe...
vith, what you eat and you choose the consequences of those choices. It's up to...
mance People make a habit of doing things that unsuccessful people find uncomfortable.
have met thousands of amazing people with AWESOME natural talent. Yet few of them fulfil th...
many never even recognise their gifts. They simply go unused. [illegible] most people appear t...
I would call NEAR LIFE EXPERIENCES. They are always about to make the big change, but som...
o busy. They think they will get round to doing it TOMORROW. If anyone ever says 'I'll start m...
morrow', or 'I'll give up smoking next week' they are not committed. If it's worth doing it's wo...
IWIN Disease (I Want It Now) You know this isn't rocket science. The things that make a real ...
ur life are remarkably easy to understand and they're well within your grasp right now. But th...
ch: Most of us are 'bone idle'. Have you noticed how many people seem to want an easy rou...
nd financial freedom? They will happily buy a product called Slim Quick because they are co...
esolve their weight problems, yet deep down they know that slimming is a combination of d...
support, discipline, drive and motivation. It takes time to reach a target weight, to adjust a me...
nge a lifestyle. And even though they know that all this EFFORT AND HARD WORK will probab...
diovascular risks and give them more energy for a longer life, they still buy Slim Quick. Come...
n't daft, just lazy!!! It's up to you High Performance People make a habit of doing th...
nsuccessful people find uncomfortable. It's up to you 80/20 I expect you will have he...
0/20 theory beforeIn simple terms it says that 80% of profits, results, inventions or whatever co...
% of the population. This law holds true in every environment I have encountered through my...
ure. When I run my seminars, after the students have had three days learning motivational an...
as on performance, I ask the following question: Based on Pareto's law I know that only 20% ...
y do anything different when you leave this seminar. Show me by raising your hand if you wil...
%. Guess what? Every hand goes up. Yet I know that the law will hold true. 80% will do nothing...
will do diddlysquat. Every day, thousands of books like this one are bought (though not read...
ple listen to CDs and attend seminars all the time, yet very few of them actually do anything c...
lt. Why should this be? As I said earlier, WE CRAVE FOR SOMETHING MORE. But somehow w...
hered to go and get it. It's somehow easier to settle for what we have and live a NEAR LIFE e...
er this: You will probably live for 80 years based upon current medical developments. If you l...
ou really want for the rest of your life how will you feel? If the Pareto Principle is true then you...
e an effort if you want to be in that 20%. A bit of effort is all it takes. And you may spend the r...
enjoying even more happiness and fulfilment, which you deserve by the way. It's up to you...
ne idle' It's up to you I was recently on holiday in France and spent some time with the M...
pany. Peter was only 21 but was easily the most professional holiday company repre...
d developed a problem with the brakes and Peter had willingly gone the ...
himself to organise a swift service at a good price. On the w...
he first joined his company when he had been just 18...
a posh suit so he would look his best (the...
d prepared a file of his achieve...
all the questions and...
As he wait...

Why you should read this chapter:

- Principally because it is important to understand how your **moods and behaviour will significantly influence your results**.
- Because **people treat you the way you teach them to**.
- Because **the way you act affects those around you**.

This final chapter is all about the way you behave. We have talked a lot about attitude, ways of thinking and creating motivational plans and goals. But it is just as important to recognise and assume the role and behaviours that will serve you best. You know what a difference it makes when you 'walk your talk'. When you act like a star you become a star. Behaving as if you are achieving your goals will really help you on your way.

And the best part of all this is that you do have control over your own behaviour. No-one has more control than you do, in fact, so it's not that hard to change your behaviour. You will soon find that shifting behaviour can also shift your attitude and mood.

Test this out. Try this experiment now (just for a bit of fun). When I ask my audience to do this on my High Performance Workshops it is always fascinating to observe.

I want you to sit in your chair and assume the posture and physiology that you would if you were completely bored! Bored out of your skull.

Do it now!

Notice how you moved. You may have slumped in your chair or dropped your head. Notice your facial muscles, how your facial expression changes.

Now . . .
I would now like you to assume the position that you would adopt if you were elated, excited and full of energy. Think of the last time you were on a real high. What does your body do now?

Notice the difference. You probably sit much more upright, smile more, raise your shoulders - even breathe differently. Some people shout out loud or whoop for joy when they feel this good.

Why do you think your body was able to move into those positions so easily? It's funny isn't it how your body understood my request so easily, yet the states I asked you to adopt were very different.

The truth is your body has rehearsed many unique physiological states to suit your moods and emotions. It has had a lot of practice! You might even have noticed how moving about actually changed your mindset? When you sat up straight you felt more positive than when you were slumped in your chair.

When I talk to top sports men or women they often talk about how they dress in athletic clothing, read athletic magazines, mix with top athletes and watch the very best performers in their field. Well before they themselves hit the big time they are 'Acting As' the very best do.

It's not what you say

High performance people understand that what they say carries far less weight than what they do.

Any parent reading this will understand this principle instantly.

Children are far more likely to reproduce an observed behaviour, than to respond to whatever their parent or teacher tells them to do. For example, if your child watches you having a glass of wine at the end of each working day and then you tell him not to start drinking because it is bad for his health, your words will have little impact. The saying 'don't do as I do, do as I say' is well known for its irony.

Equally, this leadership principle can be seen in action every day in the business world, because:

You get what you model

In other words your behaviour creates similar behaviour in others.

I was recently working with a team of managers on a two-day programme. The day started at 9 o' clock in the morning. Each day only 10 out of the 15 participants managed to turn up on time. The others arrived about 15 minutes late. Both days the same five people were late.

On the second day, we were talking about team building and team performance and the power of effective leaders. I decided to talk about punctuality and asked if any of the managers ever had a problem with lateness in their departments. I wondered if they found that reports were often handed in late. They all agreed that this was a frustrating problem.

Next, I asked if they found that their staff had a habit of being late for meetings. It so happened that not only was time keeping a problem for them but also they could actually think of the culprits' names. Some of them even rolled their eyes in disgust as they thought of the consistent offenders.

Guess which of these managers were the ones who experienced the most time keeping problems in their departments? Of course, it was the same five who had been late for our course! These five had already modelled to me that they thought lateness was acceptable.

I had no reason to assume that their lack of punctuality was an exception. After all, they had been late on both days. More than likely they behaved in this way at work too - and their team was simply doing the same. These unpunctual managers were teaching their team accepted performance standards. The power of your behaviour to influence is huge, whether you are a teacher, a parent or a manager.

When the behaviour of your subordinates frustrates you, it is likely that their behaviour is a direct reflection of what you do yourself.

People will TREAT YOU the way YOU GIVE THEM PERMISSION to.

High Performance People are acutely aware of this.

Dr Philip McGraw, who is Oprah Winfrey's coach and now has a TV programme of his own, was coaching a couple on the very delicate and serious issue of wife beating.

The man he was interviewing had beaten his wife many times during their marriage and you can imagine as the couple sat on stage with Dr Phil, how the audience were responding as they heard the story unfold. The scene was very uncomfortable.

Then Dr Phil asked a powerful and direct question of this wife beating husband.

'Why did you beat up your wife?'

There was an uncomfortable pause and then he responded.

This I will never forget.

'Because she let me,' he said.

Every time he beat her, the next day she was still there and the message he received was that beating her must be acceptable.

I don't tell this story to get into the whys and wherefores of domestic violence but the message is an important one. I'm sure you get my point.

The way you behave teaches others around you how to treat you. Before you can create yourself a success strategy you need to take a good look at yourself.

Look at yourself

I came across this quote a few years ago. It was written almost 900 years ago and can be found in the crypts of Westminster Abbey.

> *When I was young and free and my imagination had no limits, I dreamed of changing the world. As I grew older and wiser, I discovered the world would not change, so I shortened my sights somewhat and decided to change only my country.*
>
> *But it too seemed immovable.*
>
> *As I grew into my twilight years, in one last desperate attempt I settled for changing only my family, those closest to me, but alas, they would have none of it. And now, as I lie on my death bed, I suddenly realise.*
>
> *If I had only changed myself first. Then by example I would have changed my family. From their inspiration and encouragement, I would then have been able to better my country and, who knows, I may even have been able to change the world.*
>
> *Dan Clarke, Weathering the Storm*

This quote highlights a primary insight into personal leadership.

Model what you want

In Dec 2001 The Harvard Business Review had a feature on leadership. The quote on the front cover of the magazine said it all:

'Why knowing yourself is the best strategy now'

The importance of knowing yourself and understanding how your behaviour influences others is something that high performers are acutely aware of. The Westminster Abbey quote captures the Model What You Want principle brilliantly.

Changing the world would be daunting to say the least, but even if your goal is to change your career you still need to take a good hard look at yourself.

Think back to Chapter One, 'It's Up To You'. You are accountable. Too many people want something magical to happen in their lives and yet will not assume responsibility. It's not their fault. No the blame lies with their boss, their upbringing, the weather or anything - except them.

Playing the victim will help you to justify your situation but it won't change it. If you skipped Chapter One please go back and read it. It is a prerequisite to behavioural change.

Chain of influence

First look at yourself and take action. If you do so with integrity and honesty you will gain support and momentum. Eventually you will be able to influence the greater community.

The influence chain looks like this:

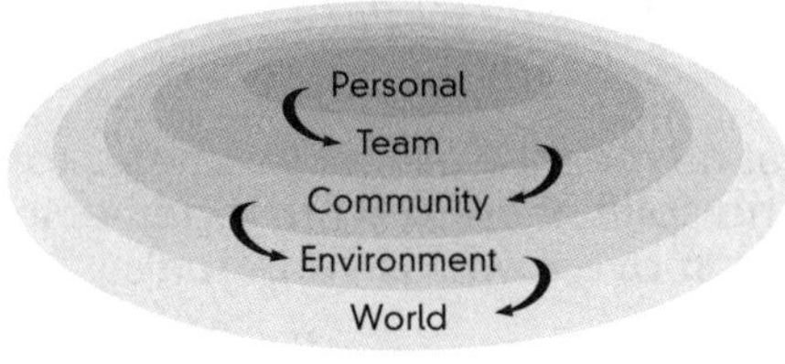

To activate this chain reaction you must exhibit some consistent value based behaviours, as listed in the chain, below:

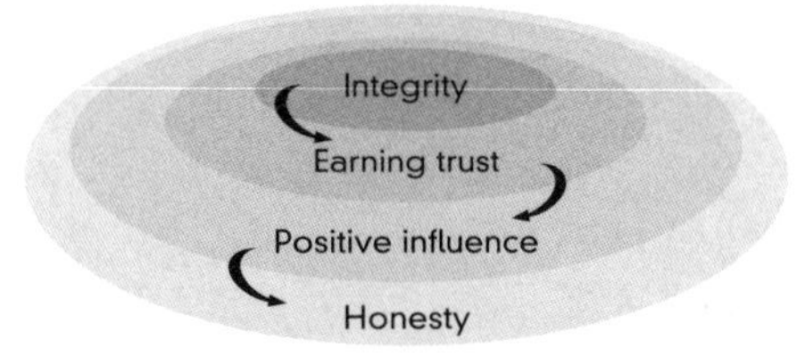

Being in integrity makes you healthier

A few years ago I was in the USA attending a National Speakers' Convention. I attended many sessions and was privileged to hear a Yale Trained Psychiatrist speaking on the subject of truth. His talk was mesmerising.

Dr Carl Hammerschlag told a wonderful story of his journey to define truth like this:

He had been travelling in Belize near the Guatemalan Border and created an opportunity to meet with a 93 year old tribal healer.

Using a translator he asked the following question: 'What's the most important thing you've learned that allows you to heal people'?

'Not to take a cold drink on an empty stomach on a hot day,' came the response via the translator.

Hammerschlag was confused by this response and asked the question again, yet received the same response:

'Not to take a cold drink on an empty stomach on a hot day.'

Eventually Hammerschlag understood the meaning:

'You can't heal people if you come to them with bad belly.'

In other words what he meant was that you need to get in balance. Your mind, body and spirit need to work together in unison before you can even start to move towards your goals.

Which means that your . . .

- Heart
- Lips
- Mind
- Actions
- Feelings

. . . are all in alignment.

So the wise old healer meant that all that you feel, believe, say, think and do must be in alignment. Only then you can operate with integrity and authenticity. Hammerschlag uses this story to define TRUTH

Operating this way feels good. When you operate without integrity or alignment it can actually make you ill. What's more people will notice your lack of authenticity.

Black clouds

Working with an audience of team leaders once, we found ourselves discussing influence and performance. As the subject evolved, one of the delegates said that she had a boss who brought a big black cloud with him every time he walked into the room of their open plan office.

'How does this make you feel?' I asked.

The Team Leader deflated in her chair and sighed heavily. This was her answer:

'How many people do you have in your team?' I asked next.

'Seven,' she replied.

'So, how does your team feel?' I continued.

Again she sighed and sunk deeper into her chair as if to act out their response.

'Out of interest, whose black cloud does your team get?' I asked this time. To me, it was clear, that her black cloud was as bad as the bosses.

It would be ridiculous to suggest that you can avoid such influences as the 'Black Cloud' manager, but you do have a choice as to how you respond. You can accept that this is the way things are and ignore it, or you can infect other people with the same negative behaviour by passing it on. Alternatively, a High Performance Person might choose to create a more effective behaviour that will create far better results for you and those closest to you.

In the book, '*Primal Leadership*', Daniel Goleman writes about this very phenomenon.

'In 1981, Psychologists, Howard Friedman and Ronald Riggio found that completely non verbal expressiveness can affect other people. For example when three strangers sit facing each other in silence for a minute or two the most emotionally expressive of the three transmits his or her mood to the other two-without a single word being spoken.'

Within groups this effect also holds true. Studies have shown that within two hours whole groups of people will end up sharing moods.

The take home message is clear. You must be aware of your moods, emotions and behaviours if you want to create encouraging, positive and ultimately high performance environments.

Equally, you need to be aware of the negative draining influences around you (psychic vampires or Mood Hoovers) and either change them or distance yourself.

Remember this whole book is about high performance and making your life work even better. It is designed to help you become more content and fulfilled. People who strive for a better life tend to be in control and simply do not accept things as they are. High Performance People certainly would challenge any negative influence and where possible distance themselves from it.

Being authentic

If there is one thing that could slow you down on your journey it's living life out of alignment with who you really are. Back to the wise words of the 93 year old healer, mentioned earlier.

You see, other people are pretty perceptive and can spot falseness a mile off.

The following exercise is possibly the most important that you will do. It will help you to find your own authentic self.

I would like you to write down your top 10 values in this space. These are the things that you value the most right now. You may write 'Health' or 'Well Being', you may write 'My Wife' or 'My Husband', 'Love' or 'Family', 'Travel' or 'Sport'.

1____

2____

3____

4____

5____

6____

7____

8____

9____

10_______________________________________

Now look at the list you have written and pick out the top four. The four things you value most. Just four. This will be the absolutely vital, the most important, can't-live-without, most precious values in your life.

My top four values

1____

2____

3____

4____

Notice how hard it can be to let some values go.
Now, I would like you to look carefully at these four values.

Get your diary and look at the amount of time you have dedicated to these values over the past six months. Look at the amount of time you have actively planned to spend on the things you value most. It is interesting how our actions often don't match up to our apparent value system, isn't it? This is sometimes the cause of frustration and lack of fulfilment.

For example, many people on my workshops write 'Health' as a Number One value. Then they spend the whole three-day programme drinking 25 cups of coffee, nine full cream deserts and avoid the gym like the plague.

Hyrum Smith, one of the leading authorities on life and time management, talks about people's 'inner governing values'. His organisation, Franklin Quest, have researched this for three decades. People who live in alignment with those things that have the highest priority in their lives almost always feel happier and more fulfilled. What's more decisions become easier because they set their goals in alignment with their values and this results in a greater sense of purpose and inner peace.

A survey conducted by Franklin Quest in 1992 asked people to list their most important values. These were then clustered into groups and ranked (this was a US survey but I think the results are relevant to all).

The top 10 values

1. Spouse
2. Financial security
3. Personal health and fitness
4. Children and family
5. Spirituality and religion
6. A sense of accomplishment
7. Integrity and honesty
8. Occupational satisfaction
9. Love for others
10. Education and learning

Living authentically means living in alignment with your personal values. It means being in integrity.

Many people find this kind of exploration a revelation and I have actually had people write to me telling me that during my training they left the room to phone a loved one to tell them 'I love you' when the realisation hit them that they have not acted the way their guiding inner values would indicate.

When you know what you value and know what you want, you need to just do it, as Nike says so aptly.

One morning at breakfast I asked Christopher (then five years old) what his Daddy valued.

His response was honest and simple.
'Well you love me, and you love golf,' he said.

Then he paused.
'And you love Mummy and you love Anna,' he continued.

I was so pleased he didn't put my job at the top of his list. Of course I do love my job, but when I first started my business I found myself working far too hard. I was busy, I was earning good money and things were going well. But one day Abby sat me down and told me things were not working. I was never there. The children never saw me. I had no time for the family. So I pledged to only work between 80 and 100 days a year. In 2003, I worked exactly 100 days. 2004 will be the same.

My job may be important to me and I value it. But if Christopher had put my job at the top of his list, I would have failed. I value my role as a dad and husband but simply saying that I value these roles is not enough.

Words are just words when there are no actions to back them up

Behavioural change

This chapter has dealt with the importance of knowing yourself and mastering your own behaviour. Because your actions significantly influence the actions of others, in other words, you get what you model. This next piece looks at the three core building blocks of Habitual Behaviour.

So let's examine these three elements. I've labelled them KSD.

K **Knowledge.......**
You know what needs to be done. This is the what.

S **Skill......**
You have the skill to apply your knowledge. This is the how.

D **Desire.....**
The D can stand for many things. Desire, Drive or Determination to apply that knowledge. This is the why.

The D can also stand for Discipline. Either way it is about a mind set towards achieving more powerful and effective behaviour.

Model what you want

When I was head of Sales Training at Bayer Pharmaceuticals some 95 per cent of all training that was offered to me from outside suppliers focused on the what and the how and either completely omitted the why or gave little attention to it. Yet, without the motive or a reason to shift behaviour the likelihood is that you will fail.

For example, let's say you want to give up smoking. You know the what because you know what needs to be done - you need to stop smoking cigarettes. You know how to do it, because you have read the books - you know you need to change the environments that have you reaching for the fag packet, you need to remove temptation, and so on.

But unless you know why you want to give up smoking, and are committed to that, you are unlikely to succeed. What are the consequences of stopping and equally what are the consequences of continuing? Ask yourself those questions to uncover your motivation to succeed, or fail.

I was recently on holiday in France. We were on the beach relaxing and the lady next to us was reading a book called 'How to Stop Smoking'. She was actually smoking a cigarette as she read! I wished I'd had my camera. It was a comical scene.

Realistically, I can't imagine her succeeding in her quest. Can you? If you want to shift a behaviour, long term, you have to cover all three bases of KSD.

The power of words (or the lack of them)

Did you know that just 7 per cent of what we communicate to other people is derived from the words we use?

And 38 per cent comes from our tone, from the way we say something.

Then a further 55 per cent comes from body language. So you see more than half of our communication is non-verbal. This puts a lot of pressure on us to BE IN INTEGRITY with what we say. If we don't, our body language and tone will let us down every time.

In practical terms, we know that the messages we receive subliminally are extremely powerful.

Model what you want

Sometimes you meet someone for the first time and, well, you just can't put your finger on it, but there is something not right about that person. Your instinct is usually right.

If you don't feel trusting towards someone, intuitively, you probably shouldn't trust him or her. If something is lacking in the visual representation of a person, then you can tell, whatever words they use when they communicate.

Here is a story to illustrate this very clearly:

We all know that communication is mostly a physical experience. People pick up the signals behind the meaning. There is a book called '*Teaching your Children Values*' by Richard and Linda Ayres. Richard and Linda are an American couple with nine children, so I guess they know a fair bit about raising kids.

One day, Linda was walking through a shopping mall. She saw a mother with her two children, a boy and a girl, about two and five years old. The children were annoying each other and making a noise, as children do, particularly when they are bored.

All of a sudden the mother could not take it any more. She stopped walking, turned round and grabbed the five year old boy and spanked him hard.

'I'll teach you to hit your sister,' she shouted.

It's so obvious, isn't it? The mother was doing just that. Her behaviour was teaching her son to keep on hitting his sister.

We can see examples like this in all walks of life. It's not what we say, but the way that we say it, that has the impact.

I'll leave you here with your sixty second summary before moving onto the final chapter that will share my story and show you how I walk my talk.

And so . . .

Words are just words when there are no actions to back them up.

se what you ...
at you eat and you cho[ose] ...
oices. So here's the thing. This bo[ok] ...
ou unless you categorically agree with both ...
ou don't agree now and know that you never will, then y...
down and go off and do something else... Still here? Excellent! Th...
set of the few - the High Performance mindset that is guaranteed to set you ...
ent, achievement and happiness. It's up to you What's in it for you? This book will ...
s that have been proven to make a difference in individual and team performance. And becau...
on't find High Performance natural we have to be disciplined to apply what we learn and take ...
et something else straight right up front. If you want an easy ride to a better richer life STOP R...
ok NOW and accept that what you have is what you will probably end up with . . . . The ideas I...
e in theory but clearly if they were all so easy to implement everyone would be doing them, w...
d they're not. All HIGH PERFORMING, successful PEOPLE that I have met or read about, WORK ...
LLY REALLY HARD. This stuff is not quick fix. PMA Mohammed Ali was one of the world's great ...
n. He was possibly the definitive world champion boxer. Many remember Ali as cocky, even a...
tistical. They thought he was a cheeky young man who talked a good game. In a recent docu...
coach recently said that the sportsman was the hardest working boxer he had ever met BOTH ...
F THE RING. He trained harder, practised more and of course had INCREDIBLE self-belief. Ali ha...
just PMA, which stands for Positive Mental Attitude, by the way. Do you think PMA is a good t...
you do. So do I. But ... be honest, here. Having a PMA does not guarantee success. For ex...
cided to run in the 100m ... Olympics right now, with no specific training, it would not ...
all the PMA in the world, you ... unlikely to win. But with PMA you would probably ...
loser. PMA is part of the deal but it is ... answer to your problems. It's up to y...
e chief executive of your life. That means ... you do. who you spe...
ith, what you eat and you choose the consequences ... choices. It's up to y...
ance People ... doing the things that unsuccessful people find uncomfortable.
ave met thousands ... people with AWESOME natural talent. Yet few of them fulfil the...
many never even recognise their gifts. They ... go unused. In fact, most people appear to ...
would call NEAR LIFE EXPERIENCES. They ... to make the big change, but some ...
busy. They think they will get round to doing it TOMORROW ... ever says 'I'll start my ...
orrow', or 'I'll give up smoking next week,' they are not committed ... doing it's wo...
WIN Disease ... You know, this is not rocket science. The thing ... make a real d...
r life are remarkably easy to understand and they lie well within your grasp right now. But the ...
: Most of us are 'bone idle'. Have ... many people seem to want an easy rou...
d financial freedom? They will happily buy ... Slim Quick because they are co...
esolve their weight problems, yet deep down they know ... is a combination of de...
support, discipline, drive and motivation. It takes time to reach a target weight, to adjust a me...
ge a lifestyle. And even ... that all this EFFORT AND HARD WORK will probabl...
iovascular risks and give ... for a longer life, they still buy Slim Quick. Come ...
't daft, just lazy!!! It's up to you High Performance People make a habit of doing th...
successful people find uncomfortable. ... 80/20 I expect you will have hea...
/20 theory beforeIn simple terms it says that 80% of profit results ... intentions or whatever co...
of the population. This law holds true in every environment I have encountered through my ...
re. When I run my seminars, after the students have had three days learning motivational and ...
s on performance, I ask the following question: Based on Pareto's law I know that only 20% o...
do anything different when you leave this seminar. Show me by raising your hand if you will ...
Guess what? Every hand goes up. Yet I know that the law will hold true. 80% will do nothing ...
ill do diddlysquat. Every day, thousands of books like this one are bought (though not read r...
le listen to CDs and attend seminars all the time, yet very few of them actually do anything di...
. Why should this be? As I said earlier, WE CRAVE FOR SOMETHING MORE. But somehow we ...
ered to go and get it. It's somehow easier to settle for what we have and live a NEAR LIFE ex...
r this: You will probably live for 80 years based upon current medical developments. If you N...
u really want for the rest of your life how will you feel? If the Pareto Principle is true then you ...
an effort if you want to be in that 20%. A bit of effort is all it takes. And you may spend the re...
enjoy even more happiness and fulfilment, which you deserve by the way. It's up to you N...
idle' It's up to you I was recently on holiday in France and spent some time with the M...
Peter was only 21 but was easily the most professional holiday company repre...
developed a problem with the brakes and Peter had willingly gone the e...
himself to organise a swift service at a good price. On the w...
first joined his company when he had been just 18 ...
... suit so he would look his best (he ...
... prepared a file of his achieve...
... questions and a...
... waite...

SIXTY SECOND SUMMARY

- *Change your physiology to change your mood.*
- *Your moods and subsequent behaviour affect those around you.*
- *Beware of passing on other people's black clouds.*
- *People will treat you the way you give them permission to.*
- *Re-check your values...are you practising what you preach?*
- *55% of communication is non-verbal so be careful what you model...people are watching!*

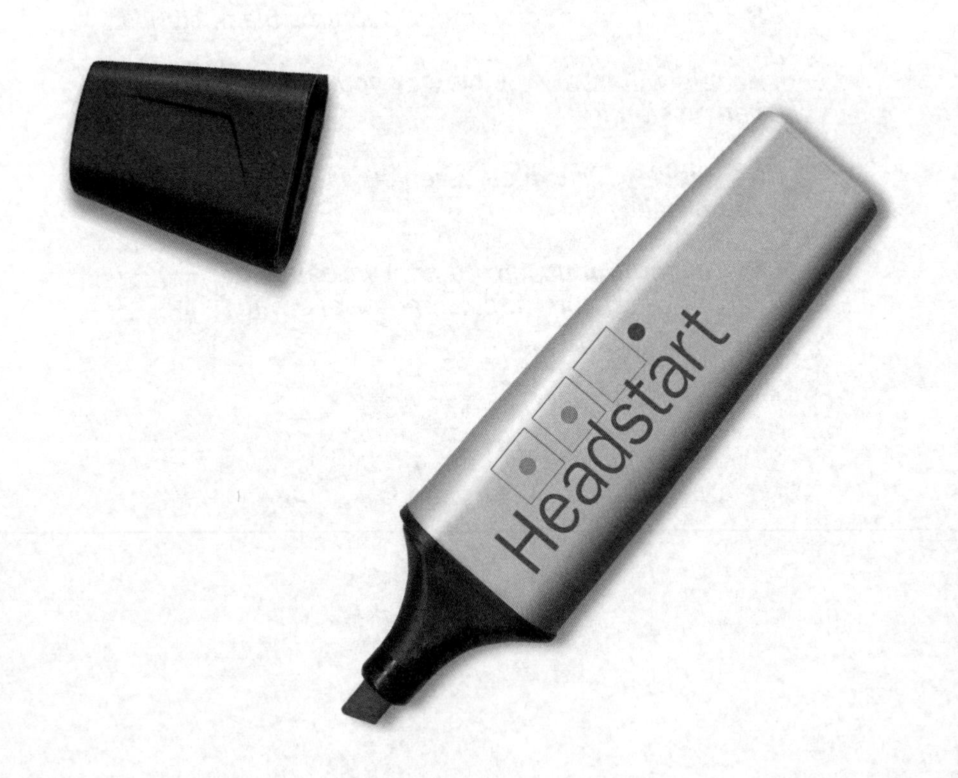
Headstart

CHAPTER 8

THE STORY OF HEADSTART

A final story

Whenever I talk to public audiences I always comment that everything I present I have applied or used in some way. It might be researched in books but I will not preach it if I am not confident that it really works.

I thought it might be helpful for you, if I outlined a living example of all of the seven themes (chapters) from this book and how their application has helped me personally.

And so I bring you . . .

The creation of Headstart

Today my business, Headstart, is just three years old. It was created in December 2001 only three months after the 9/11 disaster, which as you know, shook the world and its economy. Leaving fixed employment to create a new business always carries an element of risk but at that time the instability caused by the 9/11 incident weighed heavily on my decision to go it alone.

Three years on I have hit all financial and personal targets and my business is growing at an average of 30% per annum. I have created an opportunity to take more time (14 weeks this year, 2004) with my family and have created a debt free environment for me and my family.

Life is pretty good and the future looks bright.

When I became Head of Training and indeed as a young boy I always enjoyed talking and entertaining. My training role re-ignited my desire to present and engage an audience.

I always felt at ease in front of people. To me it was just a BRILLIANT FEELING. All the feedback I received supported the fact that I was having a positive impact and I became determined to 'do this full time'.

I was CRYSTAL CLEAR about what I wanted to become, a professional speaker and personal development trainer and coach. I KNEW WHAT I WANTED AND WHY.

I SET OUT MY GOALS. I wanted to speak to audiences about HIGH PERFORMANCE. I wanted to created shifts in behaviour to get people closer to their goals and successes.

I wanted to create a UNIQUE PRODUCT that I could offer (this was later to become Step in the Right Direction), a high performance Emotional Intelligence programme that would be tangible and practical and based upon real life experience. I met with BUSINESS COACH, Nigel Risner, who was to become pivotal to my success. I SHARED my goals and aspirations and he helped me rationalise and implement them. I knew that as keen as I was I would need HELP AND SUPPORT.

I began to SEEK OUT THE BEST speakers I could find - in fact this is how I met Nigel. I visited SEMINARS AND WORKSHOPS. I travelled to the USA to the National Speakers Association annual conference, to see the best of the best first hand. I TALKED WITH THE EXPERTS who spoke for a living and I learned everything I could about the business of speaking and the challenges of working for myself. I sought out MOTIVATIONAL FUEL.

I PRACTISED the new techniques and ideas every chance I got. I joined the PSA (Professional Speakers Association) to mix and learn and test out my skills in a public arena. I met an amazing woman called Marie Mosely. She CONNECTED me with so many talented people and gave me my first PSA presentation opportunity and has been a key member of my DREAM TEAM. I was getting ready. I was LEARNING AND LOVING IT!!!

I knew what the best were doing to be successful so I did it too. But I did it my way (as the old song says)! I recognised that it was UP TO ME to make things happen.

I had learned about mistakes and challenges made by others, so I was forewarned and forearmed. At least I would have a chance to make fewer mistakes.

I met Kriss Akabusi, who was then and still is a very successful speaker. Kriss and I began to work together and learn from each other. He was a CONSTANT SOURCE of support and positivism.

I AVOIDED ANYONE WHO DRAINED me. I could not afford practical words of wisdom like:

'Do you realise how many businesses go bust in their first year?'

'You know Steve, this is just not the right time after 9/11!'

'You must be mad leaving a 16 year career and a great job that you love so much.

The take home message is clear.

You must be aware of your moods, emotions and behaviours if you want to create encouraging, positive and ultimately high performance environments.

Don't get me wrong, these are good things to reflect on but hearing them over and over again becomes draining and I would not have left my safe job had I surrounded myself with such negative people (psychic vampires).

I MIXED WITH LIKE-MINDED, SUCCESSFUL, ESTABLISHED PEOPLE who represented probably the top 5% of the industry as I saw it. I MODELLED what I wanted.

So . . .
- I had set my goals.
- I mixed with people who were doing it really well.
- I expected success - in fact I was positive it would work.
- I knew what I wanted.
- I knew what it meant to me in terms of quality of life and creating a secure future.
- I knew that the new life was in alignment with who I was, my values my passion.
- I was practising and getting quality feedback
- I became part of a Dream Team that offered support, advice and encouragement.
- I made an effort to be like this way before I left Bayer in late 2001. I started to WALK MY TALK three years earlier, in 1998.

Abby often says that for three years I was doing two jobs, my training role for Bayer and creating the roots of a speaking business. Both as it happens were SYNERGISTIC. I was bringing creative ideas and talented people to Bayer, and thereby adding value to my role. Yet at the same time I was opening doors to my possible future. My team at Bayer in fact had a first class reputation for training so the standards we were setting professionally were second to none.

I never really knew when the BIG DAY would come but I knew it would and I felt it would be sooner rather than later. I gave up many weekends and possible relaxing mornings to attend to my new future.

August 8th 2001 Bayer announced a commercial blow that shook the organisation globally but, amazingly, this created just the opportunity I needed. I couldn't possibly have known it would happen but I was ready for it.

I remember ringing Abby and saying:

'Honey, the BUSINESS STARTS TODAY.'

These principles just work, I can't stop them working, they just do.

You can either ignore them or work with them.

It really is up to you!

When I got home that night I was greeted with a handful of business cards designed and printed by my wife. How's that for SUPPORT AND ENCOURAGEMENT?

Three months later, Headstart was born and the rest as they say, is history.

They say that luck is the result of a prepared mind and a serendipitous moment. I was prepared and the moment was right.

So, what's the headline?

These principles just work, I can't stop them working, they just do. You can either ignore them or work with them. It really is up to you!

OK THAT'S IT

This book could be 10 times longer than it is but I have attempted to pick out seven key points that when applied just seem to work.

Now that you have come to end of this book, I hope you won't go out there and tell people what you have learned or read.

Instead, I'd like you to go out and do it for yourself.

Better still, the greatest compliment you could pay me - which is also the best thing you could do for yourself - is for someone to come up to you in a few weeks' or months' time and say: 'There's something different about you. I wonder what it is.'

I wish you luck with the decisions you make.

Remember, life is not what happens to you

But what you make of what happens to you

Everyone dies, but not everyone fully lives

Too many people are having near life experiences

Knowing yourself is the best strategy now.

se what yo[u] ...
at you eat and you ch[oose] ...
ices. So here's the thing. This bo[ok] ...
ou unless you categorically agree with bo[th] ...
ou don't agree now and know that you never will, the[n] ...
own and go off and do something else... Still here? Excellent! ...
set of the few – the High Performance mindset that is guaranteed to set you ...
ent, achievement and happiness. **It's up to you** What's in it for you? This book will ...
that have been proven to make a difference in individual and team performance. And becau[se]
on't find High Performance natural we have to be disciplined to apply what we learn and take
et something else straight right up front. If you want an easy ride to a better richer life STOP RE[ADING]
ok NOW and accept that what you have is what you will probably end up with . . . The ideas h[ere]
in theory but clearly if they were all so easy to implement everyone would be doing them, w
d they're not. All HIGH PERFORMING, successful PEOPLE that I have met or read about, WORK
LLY REALLY HARD. This stuff is not quick fix. PMA Mohammed Ali was one of the world's great[est]
n. He was possibly the definitive world champion boxer. Many remember Ali as cocky, even a
istical. They thought he was a cheeky young man who talked a good game. In a recent docu[mentary]
coach recently said that the sportsman was the hardest working boxer he had ever met BOTH
THE RING. He trained harder, practised more and of course had INCREDIBLE self-belief. Ali ha[d]
just PMA, which stands for Positive Mental Attitude, by the way. Do you think PMA is a good th[ing]
you do. So do I. But let's be honest, here. Having a PMA does not guarantee success. For exa[mple]
ded to run in the 100m sprint at the Olympics right now, with no specific training, it would not
all the PMA in the world, you would still be unlikely to win. But with PMA you would probably
loser. PMA is part of the deal but it's not the answer to your problems. **It's up to y[ou]**
chief executive of your life. That means you choose what you do, who you spe[nd]
th, what you eat and you choose the consequences of those choices. It's up to y[ou]
ance People make a habit of doing the things that unsuccessful people find uncomfortable. C
ave met thousands of people with AWESOME natural talent. Yet few of them fulfil thei[r]
many never even recognise [illegible] simply go unused. In fact, most people appear to
would call NEAR LIFE EXPERIENCES. [illegible] always about to make the big change, but some
busy. They think they will get round to doing [illegible] NOW. No one ever says 'I'll start my
orrow', or 'I'll give up smoking next week,' they are not committed. [illegible] worth doing it's wor[th]
WIN Disease [illegible] You know, this is not rocket science. The [illegible] that make a real di[fference]
life are remarkably [illegible] to understand and they lie well within your grasp right now. But the[y]
: Most of us are 'bone idle'. Have you [illegible] how many people seem to want an easy rout[e]
d financial freedom? They will happily buy [illegible] called Slim Quick because they are con[vinced]
solve their weight problems, yet deep down they [illegible] slimming is a combination of de[...]
upport, discipline, drive and motivation. It takes time to reach a [illegible] weight, to adjust a met[abolism]
ge a lifestyle. And even though they know that all this EFFORT AND HARD WORK will probabl[y]
ovascular risks and give them more energy for a longer life, they still buy Slim Quick. Come o[n]
t daft, just lazy!!! **It's up to you High Performance People make a habit of doing the[...]**
successful people find uncomfortable. It's up to you 80/20 I expect you will have hea[rd]
20 theory beforeIn simple terms it says that 80% of profits, results, inventions or whatever con[...]
of the population. This law holds true in every environment I have encountered through my w[ork]
re. When I run my seminars, after the students have had three days learning motivational and
s on performance, I ask the following question: Based on Pareto's law I know that only 20% o[f]
do anything different when you leave this seminar. Show me by raising your hand if you will b[e]
Guess what? Every hand goes up. Yet I know that the law will hold true. 80% will do nothing
ll do diddlysquat. Every day, thousands of books like this one are bought (though not read n[ecessarily]
e listen to CDs and attend seminars all the time, yet very few of them actually do anything di[fferent]
Why should this be? As I said earlier, WE CRAVE FOR SOMETHING MORE. But somehow we
ered to go and get it. It's somehow easier to settle for what we have and live a NEAR LIFE ex[perience]
this: You will probably live for 80 years based upon current medical developments. If you NE
u really want for the rest of your life how will you feel? If the Pareto Principle is true then you
ar[...]fort if you want to be in that 20%. A bit of effort is all it takes. And you may spend the re[st]
enj[oying] even more happiness and fulfilment, which you deserve by the way. It's up to you M
e idle'. **It's up to you** I was recently on holiday in France and spent some time with the Ma
[...] Peter was only 21 but was easily the most professional holiday company repres[entative]
[...] developed a problem with the brakes and Peter had willingly gone the e[xtra]
himself to organise a swift service at a good price. On the wa[y]
first joined his company when he had been just 18
posh suit so he would look his best (he s[...]
prepared a file of his achievem[ents]
questions and a[...]
he waited

SIXTY SECOND SUMMARY

- *Change your Physiology to change your mood.*
- *Your moods and subsequent behaviour significently affects those around you.*
- *Beware of passing on other people's black clouds.*
- *People will treat you the way you give them permission to.*
- *Re-check your values...are you practising what you preach?*
- *55% of communication is non-verbal, so be careful what you model...people are watching!*

Learned Optimism, How to Change Your Mind and Life
Dr Martin Seligman PhD
Published by: Pocket Books

A Child Called It
Dave Pelzer
Published by: Orion

A Man Named Dave
Dave Pelzer
Published by: Orion

Emotional Intelligence
Daniel Goleman
Published by: Bloomsbury Publishing Plc

Primal Leadership
Daniel Goleman
Published by: Bloomsbury Publishing Plc

The Learning Revolution
Gordon Dryden
Published by: The Learning Web

The Seven Habits of Highly Effective People
Steve Covey
Published by: Simon and Schuster

Happiness Now
Robert Holden
Published by: Hodder and Stoughton

Teaching Children Values
Richard and Linda Ayres
Published by: Simon and Schuster

Harvard Business Review
Dec 2001 edition

Life Strategies
Dr Philip McGraw
Published by: Vermilion, an imprint of Ebony Press

Flow, The Psychology of optimal Experience
Mihaly Csikszentmihalyi
Published by: Harper and Row

Resources

Now Discover Your Strengths
Marcus Buckingham
Published by: Free Press Business

It's Not About the Bike
Lance Armstrong
Published by: Yellow Jersey Press

Taking on the World
Ellen MacArthur
Published by: Penguin

Feel the Fear and Do it Anyway
Susan Jeffers
Published by: Arrow Press

Accelerated Learning in the 21st Century
Colin Rose
Published by: Piatkus

How to Think Like a Millionaire
Mark Fisher and Mark Allen
Published by: New World Library

The 10 Natural Laws of Successful Time and Life Management
Hyrum Smith
Published by: Warner Books

Self Help
Samuel Smiles
Published by: Oxford University Press

Golf is a Game of Confidence
Dr Bob Rotella
Published by: Pocket Books

A Golden Age
Steve Redgrave
Published by: BBC

The Handbook of Emotional Intelligence
Bar on Parker
Published by: Jossey Bas

Body Language
Allan and Barbara Pease
Published by: Pease Publishing

Contact Details

To book Steve Head for your forthcoming conference or to find out more information on courses and high performance coaching.

Contact:

Headstart UK
www.headstart-uk.com
Steve@headstart-uk.com
Mobile 07774 110937
Office 01635 523 540

Comments and Suggestions

I would love to hear about your ideas, opinions and successes. Please drop me a line, I would love to hear from you.

If you would like to receive Steve's newsletter Headlines please email him and you will be included.

Clients and Programmes

Steve presents over 100 personal development workshops and seminars each year. His audiences range from school children to CEOs.

Clients include:

Academy of Chief Executives
Securicor
Master Foods (MARS)
Pfizer
Bayer Pharmaceuticals UK and Europe.
Bayer Diagnostics
Nutricia
Cow and Gate
GNC
Neways
St James Place (Rothchilds)
LHCC Managers
Northern Ireland and NHS development group
Northern Ireland NHS Finance Dept
Boehringer Ingelheim
TEC
ISMM
PSA
FAST
Astra Zeneca
Altana Pharmaceuticals
St James Place
Mundipharma
Islington Council
Easington Council
Stockton Council
Manpower INC
SW Yorkshire HA
Organon Pharmaceuticals

Courses include

Programmes

Step in the Right Direction ...3 day, Emotional Intelligence high performance workshop

VIP Leadership...helping organisations to get focused and get their teams motivated and driven.

Coach Your Way to Success...teaching high performance coaching principles to CEOs and Managers

Keynotes

What's Possible...motivational messages for kids

How to Avoid a Near Life Experience......Be inspired to make the most of your talent and Discover your Brilliance during this interactive keknote.

Steve's programmes and keynotes are entertaining and yet very practical. They are challenging and are designed to help his delegates fulfil their potential and grow.

High Performance Coaching

Steve coaches a wide range of clients from Sports Professionals to CEOs.

Testimonials

"Steve's courses are tailored specifically for our company and tangible benefits are being seen across departments where staff have attended."
Jason Brickel, Technical Director Securicor Information Systems (SIS)

"One of the best seminars I have ever had on a training event."
HFMA UK/USA conference

"Steve is an incredibly dynamic and powerful presenter and facilitator. He is also entertaining, infectiously enthusiastic, highly motivating and energetic. The feedback Steve receives from delegates on his programmes speaks for itself and I would highly recommend him as a presenter, facilitator, coach and high performance specialist."
Alison Myles, Head of training and development HFMA

Other comments

"It wasn't what I expected, but I found it insightful, emotional and I'm pleased I came"
HFMA Class Of 2004

"I have to say that Steve made the course. He stimulated and challenged me to change my perspective/attitude etc without me even realising it."
Class Of 2004

"Steve Head made this programme. Both personally and professionally"

"Steve Head provided a programme that was interesting and relevant. All the things he taught us could easily be transferred to home/social/work environments. Nothing was over complicated and it was all easily understandable."
Finance Director NHS

ose what y
hat you eat and you
oices. So here's the thing. This
ou unless you categorically agree with b
you don't agree now and know that you never will
down and go off and do something else... Still here? Excellent.
dset of the few - the High Performance mindset that is guaranteed to set y
nent, achievement and happiness. **It's up to you** What's in it for you? This book w
s that have been proven to make a difference in individual and team performance. And becau
don't find High Performance natural we have to be disciplined to apply what we learn and tak
get something else straight right up front. If you want an easy ride to a better richer life STOP R
ook NOW and accept that what you have is what you will probably end up with . . . The ideas
e in theory but clearly if they were all so easy to implement everyone would be doing them,
nd they're not. All HIGH PERFORMING, successful PEOPLE that I have met or read about, WOR
ALLY REALLY HARD. This stuff is not quick fix. PMA Mohammed Ali was one of the world's grea
en. He was possibly the definitive world champion boxer. Many remember Ali as cocky, even
otistical. They thought he was a cheeky young man who talked a good game. In a recent docu
coach recently said that the sportsman was the hardest working boxer he had ever met BOTH
OF THE RING. He trained harder, practised more and of course had INCREDIBLE self-belief. Ali h
just PMA, which stands for Positive Mental Attitude, by the way. Do you think PMA is a good
e you do. So do I. But let's be honest, here. Having a PMA does not guarantee success. For ex
cided to run in the 100m sprint at the Olympics right now, with no specific training, it would not
d all the PMA in the world, you would still be unlikely to win. But with PMA you would probabl
y loser. PMA is part of the deal but it is by no means the answer to your problems. **It's up to**
e chief executive of your life. That means you choose what you do, who you spe
ith, what you eat and you choose the consequences of those choices. It's up to y
mance People make a habit of doing the things that unsuccessful people find uncomfortable.
have met thousands of amazing people with AWESOME natural talent. Yet few of them fulfil the
many never even recognise their gifts. They simply go unused. In fact, most people appear t
I would call NEAR LIFE EXPERIENCES. They are always about to make the big change, but som
o busy. They think they will get round to doing it TOMORROW. If anyone ever says 'I'll start m
morrow', or 'I'll give up smoking next week,' they are not committed. If it's worth doing it's wo
WIN Disease (I Want It Now) You know, this is not rocket science. The things that make a real
ur life are remarkably easy to understand and they lie well within your grasp right now. But the
h: Most of us are 'bone idle' Have you noticed how many people seem to want an easy rou
nd financial freedom? They will happily buy a product called Slim Quick because they are co
esolve their weight problems, yet deep down they know that slimming is a combination of d
support, discipline, drive and motivation. It takes time to reach a target weight, to adjust a me
ge a lifestyle. And even though they know that all this EFFORT AND HARD WORK will probab
diovascular risks and give them more energy for a longer life, they still buy Slim Quick. Come
n't daft, just lazy!!! **It's up to you High Performance People make a habit of doing th**
nsuccessful people find uncomfortable.It's up to you 80/20 I expect you will have he
0/20 theory beforeIn simple terms it says that 80% of profits, results, inventions or whatever co
of the population. This law holds true in every environment I have encountered through my
ure. When I run my seminars, after the students have had three days learning motivational an
as on performance, I ask the following question: Based on Pareto's law I know that only 20%
do anything different when you leave this seminar. Show me by raising your hand if you will
. Guess what? Every hand goes up. Yet I know that the law will hold true. 80% will do nothing
vill do diddlysquat. Every day, thousands of books like this one are bought (though not read
ple listen to CDs and attend seminars all the time, yet very few of them actually do anything d
t. Why should this be? As I said earlier, WE CRAVE FOR SOMETHING MORE. But somehow w
nered to go and get it. It's somehow easier to settle for what we have and live a NEAR LIFE e
er this: You will probably live for 80 years based upon current medical developments. If you N
ou really want for the rest of your life how will you feel? If the Pareto Principle is true then yo
e an effort if you want to be in that 20%. A bit of effort is all it takes. And you may spend the r
enjoying even more happiness and fulfilment, which you deserve by the way. It's up to you
he idle **It's up to you** I was recently on holiday in France and spent some time with the M
any. Peter was only 21 but was easily the most professional holiday company repre
developed a problem with the brakes and Peter had willingly gone the
himself to organise a swift service at a good price. On the w
he first joined his company when he had been just 18
a posh suit so he would look his best (he
prepared a file of his achieve
all the questions and
he waite

Maybe you would like to jot down some of the things you have learned here, and will commit to doing something about:

Headstart